EXCUSE ME

CAN WE HAVE OUR COUNTRY BACK?

EXCUSE ME
CAN WE HAVE OUR COUNTRY BACK?

Suraj 'Eskay' Sriram

NIYOGI
BOOKS

Published by

NIYOGI BOOKS

D-78, Okhla Industrial Area, Phase-I
New Delhi-110 020, INDIA
Tel: 91-11-26816301, 49327000
Fax: 91-11-26810483, 26813830
email: niyogibooks@gmail.com
website: www.niyogibooksindia.com

Editor: Shiny Das/Niyogi Books
Design: Shashi Bhushan Prasad/Niyogi Books

ISBN: 978-93-81523-94-0
Publication: 2013

Printed at: Niyogi Offset Pvt. Ltd., New Delhi, India

This book is dedicated to the voiceless and powerless citizens of India who have now acquired a new identity—'the mango people'. They are the honest and hardworking men and women, who struggle within a social and political system that is sadly, stacked against them. Yet, they patiently persevere and make personal sacrifices in an effort to survive and give their children a chance for a better and brighter future.

Disclaimer

The book contains text and visuals that lampoon the ruling class and institutions that wield power in the country. I am not an activist, a commentator or a radical intellectual and I have no special agenda in being biased or critical of any specific individual or political outfit. The contents are a pure and simple gut reaction to what I have seen, read about or experienced in the country during the past seven years. Undoubtedly, they are cynical in nature and somewhat negative, but I have ensured that there is nothing offensive. Nevertheless, if any reader, for any reason, considers any part of the book objectionable, I apologise in advance, for it was never my intention to hurt anyone's sentiments.

Contents

'Saare jahan se achcha'
Hindostan hamara.'*

—Muhammad Iqbal
(Urdu poet)

(*Better than the whole world is our Hindostan)

'India is the cradle of the human race, the birthplace of human speech, the mother of history, the grandmother of legend, and the great grandmother of tradition.'

—Mark Twain

'India is a world in itself; it is too vast, too diverse for any complete description. It is in the midst of a great transformation. Indeed, even I who have lived here all my life, travelled many thousands of miles covering known places as well as those difficult of access, I who have met million upon million of our people cannot claim to have seen and understood all, or even most of this extraordinary land.'

—Indira Gandhi, in
Eternal India.

Preface

More than five decades ago, as a young cadet in the National Defence Academy, I had often marched to the beat of the military band playing the inspiring music set to the lyrics of '*Saare jahan se achcha, Hindostan hamara*'. I remember the overwhelming sense of pride and patriotism that swelled in me as I swung my arms and dug my heels, marching in formation on the parade ground. I felt proud of my country then and I feel proud of it today.

I'm proud that our land gave us Mahatma Gandhi—a beacon of hope for the oppressed, not only here in India but throughout the world. Then there was Indira Gandhi who made us proud by showing the world she was no pushover leader of a developing country. I remember Mark Twain, who in his own inimitable style, gave us reasons to be proud of our rich heritage. There are numerous scientists, engineers, doctors, writers, artists, industrialists and many others who, over the years, have truly reflected the greatness of our country.

For me today, the greatness of India lies in the way its enlightened citizens interact with each other. Despite the diversity in language, religion, dress, food habits, customs, and physical appearance, we make every effort to remain a unified country. This remarkable ability to remain united, despite internal and external divisive forces trying to destroy our unity, has often baffled many outsiders.

For us Indians, our unity in diversity also affords us the chance to savour limitless varieties of food, dress in a whole range of exotic outfits, and be exposed to different genres of music. Not surprisingly, girls in the south wear salwar kameez and people in the north eat idli and sambhar. Rasgullas are enjoyed as a lip-smacking dessert everywhere. *Dhokla* is often found on dining tables across the country. Bollywood has ensured that whether it is the bhangra dance, the qawwali songs, or Sufi music—they are enjoyed by one and all. Movies centred on characters from different communities spread the message of tolerance and unity. Sure, over the years we've had a few hiccups, but we have survived the misguided attempts of some communal separatist elements that threatened our unity. Past leaders of the country showed determination and resolve and dealt with these evil forces in a firm manner and thereby preserved our unity. These were my thoughts and views when I left the country about three decades ago.

Back now in India, the news that I see on TV or read in the papers is a bit disturbing. Something is amiss. It appears that people in power in every sector of governance, have failed to exploit the great potential of the nation by their ineptitude, ignorance, indifference, and dishonesty. Apart from their failures on the economic front, the country's leadership has allowed communal and divisive political entities to rear their ugly head.

Leaders of some ragtag political outfits are openly preaching hate among communities and thereby threatening the unity of the country.

To grab and retain political power at any cost, these tinpot pseudo-leaders are brainwashing gullible citizens into believing that regional pride transcends national pride. Their foot soldiers indulge in destructive behaviour and openly challenge the law enforcement agencies. I fail to understand why such shameless leaders are not arrested on charges of sedition and thrown behind bars.

Ignoring the failings of the central leadership, whether accidental or deliberate, to combat these divisive communal forces cannot be overlooked. People in power must be held accountable for their failures. To do so is our patriotic duty. In a mature democracy the views and voices of concerned citizens, in whatever form, must be heard and not silenced. Whether it is in the form of street protests, media interaction, or through cartoons and satire, we must raise our voices to express our anguish.

It is understandable that pride in one's mother tongue, traditions, and the religious customs of different communities must be protected and preserved, but regional or communal identity must not come in the way of our national identity.

With the pulls and pressures that diversity creates, there are bound to be problems among different sections of the population that appear to defy resolution. But whatever be the issues of concern to us and whatever are the solutions we seek, we must never forget that we are proud Indians first, always and every time. Only with such a mindset reconciliation between communities and harmony in the country can be achieved and maintained.

Let us rediscover the collective pride and nationalistic spirit we all had at the time of our Independence, and together, help save our country from the downward and divisive spiral of regionalism and communalism.

Jai Hind.

Introduction

On my return to India in 2005, after having spent about twenty years abroad in the US, I was amazed to see the phenomenal changes that had taken place in the country since my departure in 1985. Glitzy malls, imposing high-rise offices and flats, upscale hotels and restaurants, and vast networks of flyovers were everywhere. Luxury cars on the roads were dime a dozen. Everyone on the road, or in a car, or in a shopping centre, was moving around with a cell phone glued to the ear. WOW! Had India changed or what!

As a political cartoonist, one is conditioned to look beyond the obvious. As I once again settled in the country, I sensed that beneath the external sheen that blinded the senses, lurked a dark secret. The spotlight of 'India Shinning' shone only on a privileged few. The greatness the country bragged about as *'Mera Bharat Mahan'* was a selective slogan. Life for a vast majority of the Indian population was still a struggle against corruption, poor living conditions, a degraded environment, galloping inflation, and a host of other ills. Most of these problems were a direct result of ill-conceived and often divisive policies, coupled with poor governance and abysmal administration at all levels.

Though I don't qualify as a typical *aam aadmi*, or 'mango people' as some would prefer to call that section of the population, my years of being a cartoonist have conditioned my thought process in a manner that I am able to see life through the eyes of the real *aam aadmi*.

After seven years of observing and experiencing life in urban India, I felt a sort of compulsion to share my thoughts with the reading public. Hence this book.

India is a complex country. The resolution of the diverse problems the *aam aadmi* faces is a daunting challenge.

In this book, I have tried to highlight those issues that have had a negative impact on my adjustment back into the country after an extended absence. Some things made me angry, while some hurt my conscience. I felt the country had been hijacked by politicians, bureaucrats, law enforcement agencies, builders, and others of their ilk. Enormous power and authority, whether constitutional or not, had been usurped by these people and the common man was at their mercy.

The democratic institutions of the world's largest democracy had been twisted and perverted. The evolution of 'dynasties' and vote banks have had a direct impact on the electoral process, giving rise to election victories of known criminals and local goons. They in turn corrupt the babus, cops, developers, and builders to an extent that the quartet pretty much own the country and the souls of its hapless citizens.

In all fairness, I must state that the *aam aadmi* too is not entirely blameless. Our indifference has been instrumental in the election of scoundrels to political office, the degradation of the environment, and the lack of civic behaviour. Some have also allowed themselves to be brainwashed by radical militant outfits or religious bigots who are out of tune with the aspirations of modern India. Religion is something between you, your God and your place of worship. It has no place in politics or governance.

There are no easy answers or solutions to ridding the country of the rot that has set in at all levels of governance. All that the common man can take solace in is the hope that the current political *kalyug* will pass soon and there will emerge a charismatic messiah who will lead the people to a better and brighter future.

Keep hope alive.

Who are 'We'?

Leaving aside politicians, bureaucrats, defence personnel, and the police force, who are a class apart, the people of this great country range from the business tycoons who flaunt their Rolls Royces and live in five-star luxury to the poor farmer who is driven to suicide for want of some assistance to feed his starving family. Between these two limits are the multitudes who exist at various socio-economic levels and who bear the brunt of inefficiency, corruption, and poor governance in their daily lives. These are people who, facing a system that is insensitive to their needs, spend their time, energy, and their waking moments struggling to provide the basic necessities of *roti, kapda aur makaan* (food, clothing and shelter) for themselves and their families.

The educated lot, by virtue of possessing better employment potential, faces a lesser struggle. They can aspire to a better quality of life. Then, there are a large number of those who have missed the opportunity of getting some form of education, or else, having gone through a dismal public school system, are functionally illiterate. They make up for their lack of education by working hard at semi-skilled or unskilled jobs, or subsistence farming. They are all loyal citizens of the country and all they long for is a living wage, decent housing, decent schools, easy transportation, clean water, reliable electricity, a safe environment and above all, good governance.

This is who 'We' are.

Eskay

Who Has Taken Our Country?

Any institution, group or authority that harasses and makes life difficult for the honest and hardworking citizen is guilty of having stolen the country. Whether it is the corrupt, egotistical, and ineffective politician, the obstructionist bureaucrat, the graft-taking policeman, or the dishonest developer/builder—they are all party to the theft.

Then there the many homegrown fundamentalist groups, regional chauvinistic outfits along with self-appointed moral brigades who, through intimidation and violence, have stolen the fundamental right of self expression guaranteed to the citizens of the country under the constitution. They revel in creating communal disharmony and thereby steal the unity of the country. Added to this list are festival organisers and event managers who, emboldened by a weak and ineffective police force, blatantly deprive people of sleep with loud music and burst fire crackers through the night with impunity.

Included as accomplices in this heist are the corrupt and uncaring officials who have allowed the industries to pollute the air, water, and soil and deprive the people of the country of a healthy living environment.

Lastly, there is the politician-developer-builder nexus. This unholy alliance has ensured that large tracts of land belonging to poor farmers are literally stolen and cities are allowed to get overbuilt without the provision of adequate infrastructure thereby depriving citizens of good roads, adequate water, electricity, and other basic services needed to lead a decent life.

They all stand accused of stealing our country.

J'accuse!!

Getting to Know Your Neta

I am a neta ...

I am a Neta
And a VVIP.
I have a lot of power;
Don't you mess with me!

I'm driven in a car,
With a flashing red light,
And a cavalcade behind me;
What an awesome sight!

Get to Know Your Neta

Neta, is a Sanskrit word the meaning of which is 'a guide', or 'a leader'. In the post-Independence political scene, India had its share of politicians who, because of their honesty, integrity, intellect, and selfless service to the country, were true netas, in every sense of the word. We recognised them, we revered them and when they passed away, we remembered them. There was something special about them that appealed to the common man. People looked up to them with pride and reposed their faith in them to lead the country in the crucial first few steps of a nascent democratic India. The following page has portraits/caricatures of some of these great netas.

Sadly, today the word neta appears to have mutated into something that has a derogatory connotation, and in most cases, invites ridicule instead of respect from the common man.

But how does one portray the enigma that is the Indian neta. Words often fail. Perhaps cartoons and satire are a better alternative.

Tab ke Neta Mahan

Mahatma Gandhi

Pandit Nehru

Sardar Patel

Subhas Chandra Bose

C. Rajagopalachari

Rajendra Prasad

Indira Gandhi

Jagjivan Ram

Lal Bahadur Shastri

Ab ke Neta Maha ...

(Fill in the Blank)

After having mentally filled in the blank in the title above with a word/ words of your choice, let us explore, in cartoons, the world of the Indian neta.

Barring a few, modern day netas are usually a breed of nondescript individuals found in various positions of political power at the centre, state, and district levels. They flaunt an image of authority by strutting around surrounded with gun-toting militia or driving around in a cavalcade flashing red lights, blaring sirens, and causing traffic jams for the hapless citizens.

It appears that they need this tamasha to satisfy a bloated ego whenever they need to show off their presence in front of 'we the people'. It's true that in these troubled times, people in positions of power need a certain amount of protection, mostly from disgruntled citizens (remember the slapping incident of a senior politico?), but the protection should be discreet and unobtrusive and not flaunted as a status symbol. Leaders should realise that strutting around with a pack of armed combatants doesn't invite awe but the scorn of the common man.

Netas at the national level get elected through a periodic ritual called elections, where a perplexed *aam aadmi* is coaxed, cajoled, extorted, and at times intimidated to vote for a current or potential neta irrespective of whether he/she is deserving of such power or authority. Most have the ability to usurp political power through groups of voters beholden to them, usually poor and living in slums, whom they protect and nurture and whose votes they draw on at election time. They are their 'vote banks'.

For most netas, having a CBI enquiry, vigilance enquiry or being arrested on serious charges and then being released on bail doesn't matter at all. They all wear a mantle of Teflon.

Netas are often seen on TV or in the print media either denying or justifying their misdeeds in a manner that most intelligent viewers/readers perceive as hollow. It is obvious that most of the responses are scripted and lack sincerity.

Candid Chat

WHY IS THE NETA CONSIDERED A MATHS GENIUS?

HE 'MULTIPLIED' HIS NET WORTH 100 TIMES IN JUST 1 YEAR.

HOW DID THE NETA REMOVE POVERTY IN HIS WARD?

BY BULLDOZING THE SLUM WHERE THEY LIVED.

HOW DOES THE NETA MANAGE TO KEEP GETTING RE-ELECTED?

DIVIDE AND FOOL.

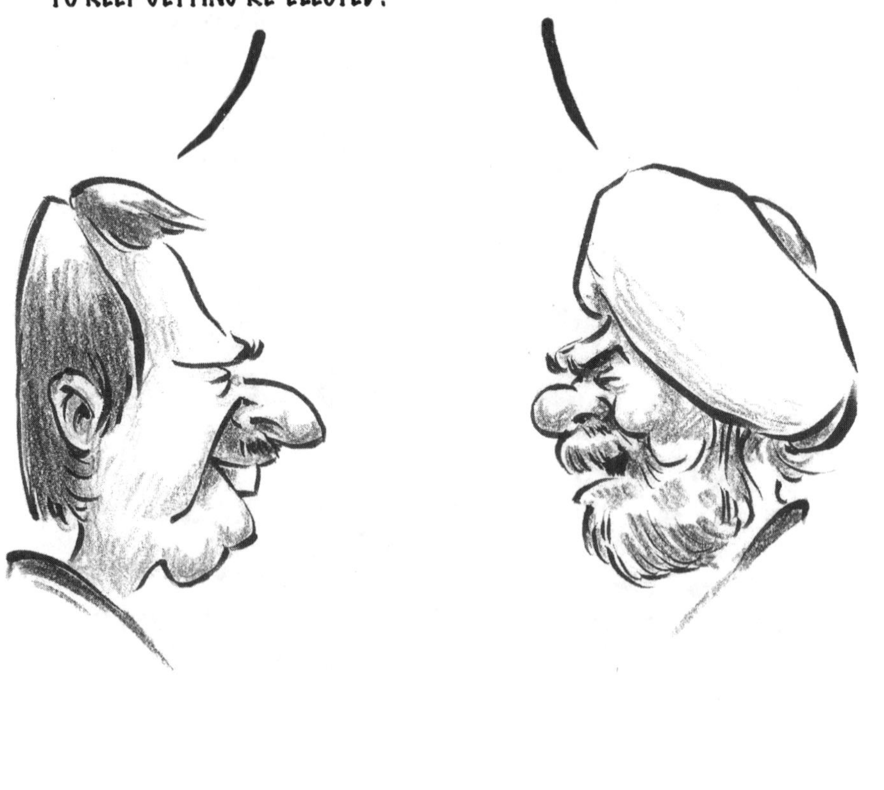

I WILL SHOW THE WORLD WHAT
AN INDIAN NETA IS CAPABLE OF DOING.
I WILL DO WHAT EVERYONE SAYS CANNOT BE DONE...
...I WILL FOOL ALL THE PEOPLE ALL THE TIME.

THE MONSOONS HAVE FAILED, THE CROPS ARE GONE, I'M FIGHTING FOR MY SURVIVAL.
MY POLICIES HAVE FAILED, MY SUPPORT IS GONE, I'M FIGHTING FOR MY SURVIVAL TOO.

BEFORE YOU VOTE, DO YOU CHECK THE NETA'S TRACK RECORD?
NO ...
... HIS POLICE RECORD.
VOTE for

Candid Chat

WHAT DID THE NETA DO WHEN THE WOMENFOLK SCREAMED AND SHOUTED AT HIM FOR NOT DOING ENOUGH FOR THE VILLAGE?

HE BROKE INTO A SONG-'WHY THIS KOLAVERI DI?'

WHAT HAPPENED WHEN YOU CALLED THE NETA AND DEMANDED TO KNOW WHY THE DREADED TERRORIST HAD STILL NOT BEEN HANGED?

HE HUNG UP.

HOW COME THE NETA NEVER MAKES MISTAKES?

WHEN YOU DO NOTHING, HOW CAN YOU MAKE A MISTAKE?

When one sees the mugshots of the candidates and their supporting chamchas in the posters and hoardings that sprout all over the city before any local or state election, one gets the feeling that the faces of the individuals belong to either a goon with a criminal record or a vagrant one encounters on city streets. In a lot of cases the public is not wrong in its assessment. The image of aspiring leaders should convey to the citizen the feeling of respect, sensitivity, honesty, and a sort of implied assurance that if elected they will work for the good of everybody. The reaction of common folks when they see the mugshots of these aspiring leaders on election posters is more like, 'Oh no! Not these fellows!'

OF COURSE WE ARE SERIOUS ABOUT ERADICATING POVERTY. SEE, WE'VE BUILT THIS NEW 50-CRORE SWANKY OFFICE JUST FOR THAT.
OFFICE OF DEPARTMENT FOR ERADICATION OF POVERTY
COULDN'T THEY JUST DISTRIBUTE THAT MONEY TO THE POOR INSTEAD?

VOTE FOR ME DEAR BROTHERS. I PROMISE LAND FOR THE LANDLESS, JUSTICE FOR THE POOR, PROTECTION OF THE WEAKER SECTIONS, BLAH! BLAH! BLAH!
BAH!! LIAR.... ..CHEAT
VOTE FOR ME MY FRIENDS. I PROMISE HOMES FOR THE HOMELESS, FOOD FOR THE HUNGRY, CLOTHING FOR THE NEEDY, BLAH! BLAH! BLAH!
BAH!! LIAR.... ...CHEAT
NOW LISTEN CAREFULLY. YOU BETTER VOTE FOR ME OR ELSE ... REMEMBER, ONCE I'M ELECTED, DON'T EXPECT ANY HELP FROM ME. I PROMISE YOU NOTHING. ALL I DO WILL BE FOR MYSELF. GOT IT?
DID YOU HEAR THAT. AT LAST WE HAVE AN HONEST MAN WHO SPEAKS THE TRUTH. SATYAMEVA JAYATE ... MY VOTE IS HIS.

Candid Chat

DESPITE HIS PROMISES, WHY HAS THE NETA NOT TAKEN THE PATH TO DEVELOPMENT?

WHERE THERE IS NO WILL, THERE IS NO WAY.

THE NETA'S ELECTION SPEECH WENT ON AND ON. DID IT MAKE ANY SENSE TO YOU?

WHEN THERE IS A GLUT OF WORDS, THERE IS A LACK OF SUBSTANCE.

AFTER THE NETA DELIVERED A SPEECH TO PACIFY THE CROWD, THEY WERE IN TEARS. WAS IT BECAUSE OF SORROW OR JOY?

TEAR GAS

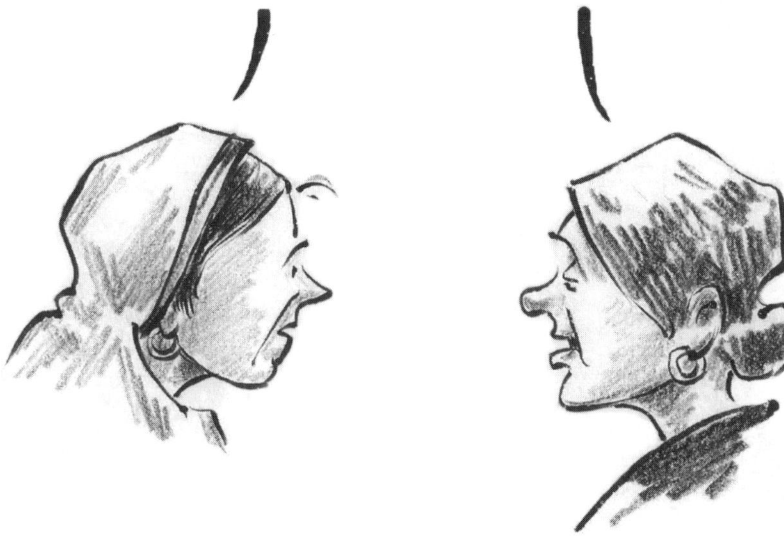

An Interview with the Neta

1. WHAT IS YOUR FAVOURITE PLANT?

   1. MONEY PLANT

2. WHAT IS YOUR FAVOURITE TV GAME SHOW?

   2. KAUN BANGEA CROREPATI

3. ARE INDIAN BANKS ANY GOOD?

   3. SWISS BANKS ARE BETTER

4. WHAT ARE YOUR VIEWS ON GREED?

   4. GREED IS GOOD ... REMEMBER WALL STREET?

5. WHAT ABOUT INTERNATIONAL RELATIONS?

   5. I HAVE PLENTY. AN UNCLE IN CANADA, TWO BROTHERS IN NEW JERSEY AND A COUPLE OF COUSINS IN DUBAI.

6. YOU CLAIM THAT YOU WILL BE AN EXCELLENT FOREIGN MINISTER. HOW SO?

   6. YOU SEE, I HAVE LOTS OF FOREIGN CARS, I MAKE LOTS OF FOREIGN TRIPS, ALL MY CHILDREN STUDY IN FOREIGN UNIVERSITIES AND LASTLY, I HAVE SO MANY FOREIGN BANK ACCOUNTS.

7. DO YOU FEEL YOU CAN BE A GOOD DEFENCE MINISTER?

   7. CERTAINLY. SEE HOW WELL I HAVE DEFENDED MYSELF IN THE NUMEROUS CORRUPTION CHARGES AGAINST ME!

8. LASTLY, THERE'S A RUMOUR THAT YOU MAY BE MADE MINISTER OF PRISONS. DO YOU FEEL UPTO THE JOB?

   8. OF COURSE. I'VE BEEN IN AND OUT OF THEM SO MANY TIMES!

NO, NO!!
HE'S NOT PROSTRATING BEFORE THE NETA ... HE'S JUST WIPING THE DUST OFF HIS SHOES.

The Rise of the Political Spokesperson

Political Spokespersons, also known as 'spin doctors' or 'spinmeisters', are designated individuals who make statements on behalf of a senior neta or a political party. They are generally oversmart and glib-tongued lawyers adept at twisting and stretching the truth so as to suit the way the establishment wants a particular issue to be conveyed to the apparently gullible public. Sometimes one feels they may have forgotten the national motto—'Satyameva Jayate'—Truth Alone Triumphs.

Reporter	**Spokesperson**
The buzz is that the neta got large, unsecured, interest-free loans for his family business from a big building contractor.	That's a lie.
It's being said that a private company sold the neta, prime land, at throwaway prices.	That's a lie.
It's been reported that the neta was gifted half a dozen luxury flats by a company perhaps as a quid pro quo for a favour done.	That's a lie.
It's rumoured that a lot of black money was involved in these transactions.	That's a lie.
The word on the street is the neta lacks the moral values expected of a leader.	That's a lie.
Some people think the neta is basically a good man.	That's a lie ... Oooops!

Candid Chat

THE NETA SPENT 5 CRORES IN HIS CONSTITUENCY. WAS IT TO REPAIR CRUMBLING SCHOOL BUILDINGS, RESURFACE ROADS, PROVIDE CLEAN WATER AND BASIC TOILET FACILITIES?

NO. HE SPENT IT ON HIS DAUGHTER'S WEDDING.

THE POOR CHILD TOLD THE NETA SHE HAD NOT EATEN ALL DAY. THE NETA ASKED HER, 'WHY? ARE YOU FASTING?' WHAT WAS HER REPLY?

NO. I'M STARVING.

WHAT DID THE NETA SAY WHEN HIS CONSTITUENTS TOLD HIM THAT THINGS WERE SO BAD, THEY COULD NOT EVEN AFFORD TO EAT 'ROTIS'?

HE SAID ... 'EAT PARATHAS THEN'.

'If a country values anything more than freedom, it will lose its freedom: and the irony of it is that if it is comfort or money that it values more, it will lose that, too.'

—William Somerset Maugham

THIS IS SABARMATI ASHRAM.
GANDHI ONCE STAYED HERE.
WHO ?
INDIRA OR SONIA ?

Hey Ram!!

Have we forgotten Bapu?

Even if not totally forgotten, Gandhiji is seldom remembered other than on his birth or death anniversary. I wonder how many people have taken note of the fact that hardly any neta sports a 'Gandhi topi' these days. Is it just a sartorial change or is it a subtle symbolic message that the vision and guiding principles by which Mahatma Gandhi inspired the people of this country, are no longer relevant in the eyes of the netas of today?

It is a travesty that this sacred land, reclaimed from the British by Gandhiji has been grabbed from the people by unscrupulous netas.

WHAT!
YOU DON'T KNOW ME?
YOU DON'T KNOW
WHO I AM?
ER ... ARE YOU
RAVANA?

Candid Chat

WHAT DOES THE STEEL CUPBOARD IN THE NETA'S OFFICE CONTAIN? SECRET FILES?

NO. SECRET CASH.

DURING THE OFFICIAL TRIP ABROAD, DID THE NETA TAKE ALONG A LOT OF HIS STAFF?

NO. A LOT OF HIS RELATIVES.

WHAT DO YOU MAKE OF NETAS CREATING AN UPROAR OVER A CARTOON PRINTED IN A TEXTBOOK?

IT'S A CASE OF CARTOONS OBJECTING TO CARTOONS.

SIR, WE NEED TO IDENTIFY NEW TECHNOLOGY TO REPAIR POTHOLES, RECYCLE GARBAGE, CLEAN THE ENVIRONMENT, SAVE ENERGY, USE RAIN WATER HARVESTING ETC. I SUGGEST FORMING A STUDY GROUP.
EXCELLENT IDEA. I'LL PACK MY BAGS FOR A STUDY TOUR TO SWITZERLAND, GERMANY, ITALY, FRANCE AND ON MY WAY BACK PERHAPS I'LL MAKE A HALT AT SEYCHELLES AND DUBAI. OKAY MAKE THE ARRANGEMENTS.

Candid Chat

WHAT ADVICE WAS THE NETA GIVEN WHEN SOMEONE IN THE CROWD SLAPPED HIM ON THE CHEEK ?

HE WAS TOLD TO BE A SPORT AND OFFER THE OTHER CHEEK TOO.

TO GET RE-ELECTED, DID THE NETA OFFER THE VILLAGERS CLEAN DRINKING WATER ?

NO. HARD COUNTRY LIQUOR.

DOES THE NETA HAVE AN ACCOUNT IN THIS COOPERATIVE BANK ?

NO. HE DOESN'T NEED TO. HE OWNS THE BANK.

YOUR HONOUR, MY CLIENTS, THE YEDDY BROTHERS, DESERVE A LIGHTER SENTENCE. AFTER ALL, THEY ARE MINORS.
OBJECTION. YOUR HONOUR, THEY ARE NOT MINORS ... THEY ARE MINERS, AND CROOKED ONES TOO.

PSST!! LATER SIR, LATER!
RIGHT NOW YOU NEED TO SAY 'HELLO'
AND EXTEND YOUR HAND LIKE THIS.

'Patriotism is supporting your country all the time, and your government when it deserves it.'

—Mark Twain

It's a Family Affair

*(Statutory Warning:
Smoking is injurious to your health.)*

'Tainted politicians with criminal records rule the roost in the political arena and don't let go of their grip on power. Who is going to dislodge them? Definitely not the current system of 'vote bank' and 'dynastic' politics. On a cynical note, maybe a 'dynastic concept' within our dysfunctional democracy be institutionalized and the constitution amended accordingly.'

Excerpt from *Indira Gandhi: The Final Chapter*

First there was one, then half a dozen, and now there seems to be scores of them. These are the political dynasties that have sprouted all over the country in the last few decades. These dynasties have amassed political and money power within a closed circle of family members, which is put to use when 'free and fair' elections take place. Wives, sons, daughters, cousins, uncles, nephews—all get on the gravy train and make sections of the country their personal fiefdom. This gentry is now the modern day 'royalty' minus the titles of yore that the princely states gave to their rulers.

They often proclaim grandiose schemes and projects, ostensibly for the good of their gullible subjects. More often than not, their hare-brained visions are just a means to siphon off money into their war chests through dubious policies and procedures.

This compulsive possessive behaviour of the patriarchs and matriarchs of these dynasties is, without question, driven by greed. Having acquired enormous wealth by greedily looting the country, they need to ensure its safe custody on a long-term basis. To this end, it becomes imperative for them to subvert the political system in a manner so as to retain political power within the family for generations to come.

The common man sees the wealth of the country gradually sucked out by this dynastic species with very little to show for good governance in return. They have become the proverbial 'white elephants'.

A pledge we would like all netas to take:

The unity, security, and development of the country comes first, always and every time.

The welfare and aspirations of the people come next, always and every time.

Your own welfare, financial or otherwise, comes last, always and every time.

(Inspired by the 'Chetwode Motto')

The Mighty Mandarins and Their Minions

I am a babu ...

I am a Babu;
Smart and bright;
Never question me,
'Cause I'm always right.

If you need an approval,
For a thing or two;
Just check with my peon;
He'll tell you what to do.

Indian officialdom exists at many levels. There are those at the very senior level who walk the halls of power in the centre and state capitals and are, by and large, highly qualified, motivated and experienced but somewhat pompous individuals. Most have remained honest and have stood by their principles, though of late some have succumbed to greed and political pressure to join the bandwagon to loot the country.

These mighty mandarins ponder over figures and statistics and after due deliberation formulate grandiose plans that are meant to help improve the quality of life of the urban and rural *aam aadmi*. Sometimes, with too much focus on statistics and numbers, they forget they are dealing with human beings in need. A classic example was the profound determination that the common man can subsist on ₹ 28 to ₹ 30 a day. My advice to them is that they need to keep their feet on the ground and get a dose of reality.

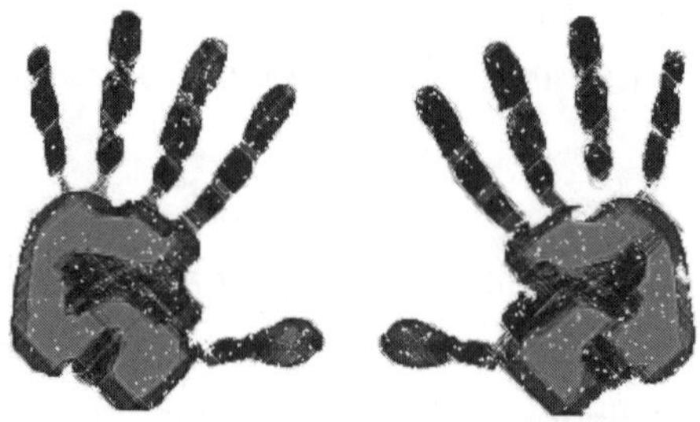

A Brief Encounter

I had just returned to the country after an absence of twenty years. Walking down the street I was accosted by a beggar woman. I offered her a few rupee coins. 'What?' screamed the woman. Glaring at me and thrusting her two hands with ten outstretched fingers in my face, she said 'Das Rupiya'—'I want ten rupees'.

It got me thinking. Even if she managed only four hits a day, she would be earning more than the government's subsistence threshold of ₹ 30. Will the bureaucracy, from now on, consider her to be not a poor beggar but a crafty extortionist living beyond her needs? Sounds silly doesn't it?

Babus at the state level are perhaps the most harried lot of bureaucrats. They are always under intense political pressure and cannot escape the influence of petty politics played out by their regional masters, who are usually a motley collection of some burnt-out and totally ineffective old timers or a ragtag bunch of semi-literate local *dadas* masquerading as netas. Their myopic vision of development and progress does little to help the babus make a difference in the lives of the citizens. They appear to accept the inevitable truth in their relation with politicians—'If you can't beat them, join them'.

Then there are babus at the district and local levels. They are those whom the *aam aadmi* has to interact with for almost all their needs. They are unfortunately the worst of the bunch. They are indifferent, incompetent, and steeped in corruption. Nothing happens till their palms are greased. Despite their position at the lowest level of 'babudom', they wield a lot of authority and the common man wanting a job done, has no option but to yield to the nefarious practice of bribery. Since the spoils of bribery are shared by one and all in a particular office, there is no incentive to curb it. People have no choice but to keep depleting their income by shelling out bribes for every little documentation, licence or certificate needed.

An idle thought comes to mind in this regard. Why not make the process of administration more transparent and officially levy a sort of nominal, fixed service charge, for all processing and approvals handled by the local babus? The money collected each month can be divided amongst the staff of that department to supplement their salary. It will be a win-win situation for all. The transparency will ensure that people are aware of the specific rates to get a job done expeditiously. The office staff will work harder to process and approve as many applications as possible and thereby take home a fatter pay cheque every month.

Any takers for this brilliant suggestion?

HORNS OF A DILEMMA

The Real VIP, Very Influential Person in Babuland

The Police Farce

I am a policeman …

I am a policeman,
Guardian of the law;
I love to see you tremble,
Haw! Haw! Haw!

I have the power,
I have the might;
If I feel you are guilty,
I'll lock you up for the night.

Are You Being Served ?

The following are some quotes I came across while surfing the Internet:

- *To Protect the Good and to Destroy the Evil*
- *Truth Alone Triumphs*
- *We Care For You*
- *Citizens First*

These are (surprise, surprise) mottoes of the police forces of some of our major cities.

The *aam aadmi* expects that the primary role of the police is to protect and serve the people of the country. However, other than at a busy road intersection, one rarely gets to sees a cop on a neighbourhood beat. Nonetheless, they mysteriously emerge from the woodwork in large numbers whenever a VIP is passing through their area of jurisdiction. Where are these cops the rest of the time?

Other than VIP visits, there are also occasions when you see hordes of policemen at major intersections during the day, or during the raid of some bar at night. Sadly, they are not there to control traffic or check on the welfare of the partygoers. Their primary objective is to trap unsuspecting suckers who may have violated some obscure law that no one follows anyway, and in the process perhaps make a quick buck.

Officers and men of the police force can be broadly classified into three categories. The first include the educated, intelligent, and motivated IPS professionals who aspire to make a difference. They are professionals of unquestionable integrity. In their zeal to effectively serve the people, they often do things that are not to the liking of their political bosses. This results in them being transferred and shunted around frequently. They often quit the service when they realise their impeccable credentials are not considered an asset.

CAN'T YOU READ ?
THIS AREA IS FOR
VVIP PARKING ONLY.
OOPS!! SORRY ... I
DIDN'T KNOW IT WAS
A 'RED LIGHT' AREA.
VVIP
Parking
Eskay

The next category includes those who accept the reality that within the constraints of political overlordship, there is not much that they can do. They would concede rather than confront. They avoid taking any initiatives that could enhance efficiency in their departments, since they know that such measures generally attract the wrath of the politicians.

Finally, we have those police personnel who early on in their careers, accept the inevitable, and adjust to the vagaries of political control on their jobs and their lives. They are more likely to serve their own interests and those of their political masters at the expense of the needs of the common folk. They allow themselves to be sucked into a world of inefficiency and corruption. With protection from politicians at the local and state levels, they are able to do pretty much what they want without the fear of any kind of disciplinary action. This is a category that the common man faces most of the time, on the streets or at the police chowki. They give the police force a bad reputation.

Against this backdrop, how can the common man expect the police force to exhibit any of the virtues so eloquently expressed in the mottoes listed earlier? In fact, recent happenings that have made the news show another disturbing trend where policemen in junior positions have deliberately ignored the directives of their superiors, and have harassed and arrested innocent citizens, violating their fundamental rights. They have allowed goondas to vandalise the property of the people, all at the behest of illiterate and uncouth goons masquerading as local leaders. It is apparent that the local police have now become the handmaidens of politicians. This is a dangerous trend and must be nipped in the bud. A politicised police force will be nothing but a nightmare for the *aam aadmi*.

Who's the Boss?

THERE GOES
MORAL POLICEMAN
INSPECTOR OGRE.
THINKS HE'S GOD.
I WONDER WHY ...
BECAUSE,
WHEN BAR DANCERS
AND PARTYGOERS
SEE HIM COMING,
THEY ALL CRY OUT
'OH GOD!'

LOOK! THERE COMES A COP.
WE'RE IN TROUBLE.
DON'T WORRY.
GANDHIJI WILL
PROTECT US.
NO
HAWKERS
ALLOWED

"WHAT DO YOU MEAN YOU COULDN'T SEE THE STOP LIGHT? IT'S RIGHT THERE IN FRONT OF THAT BILLBOARD, BEHIND THE TREE NEXT TO THE STREET SIGN.

Instead of just blaming the police, the *aam aadmi* also needs to introspect. We too must take some of the blame. When the police do try to implement the law by going after the lawbreakers, we accuse them of high-handedness or moral policing, and when they don't, we curse them for their inaction. Either way, they always come out as losers.

The police force can fulfil the aims only when they can operate in an environment that ensures complete removal of illegal or illegitimate political pressure. The police reforms that have been gathering dust for decades need to be once again reviewed by a competent committee of concerned citizens, bureaucrats, policemen and politicians, and then they need to be implemented. The powers that be need to face this lingering issue and have the guts to surmount the impediments that are sure to crop up at the behest of vested interests.

Give the policeman proper training, adequate status, respect, and your full cooperation, and I'm sure they will respond to the needs of the citizens. Then, and only then, can the farce become a force.

Cops and Goons

Building Matters

I am a builder ...

I am a builder,
With a lot of clout;
If I want your land;
Quietly move out.

The Neta and I,
Are thick as thieves;
Don't dare challenge us;
Just pack up and leave.

Like the dog in Pavlov's experiments, the Indian developer/builder begins to salivate the moment he sees a patch of open land. Their obsessive-compulsive reaction is to grab it, own it, and build on it, never mind that the plot was reserved for housing for the poor, or a school, or for a recreational facility. The builders are in cahoots with politicians and local officials, and so, rules are bent, laws are flouted, and environmental issues ignored. They have no qualms when undertaking illegal development or construction projects that block natural water bodies or even building residential properties below the surveyed flood lines.

SO, WHAT ARE THESE MITIGATING CIRCUMSTANCES I SHOULD CONSIDER TO REDUCE HIS SENTENCE?
YOUR HONOUR, MY CLIENT BUILT THE ILLEGAL STRUCTURE WITH SUCH POOR MATERIAL THAT THE CIVIC AUTHORITIES WILL NEED TO SPEND VERY LITTLE MONEY TO DEMOLISH IT.

GRANTED IT'S BEEN BUILT BELOW THE FLOOD LINE, BUT LOOK AT THE PLUS SIDE. WHEN THE WATER LEVEL RISES DURING THE MONSOONS, YOU'LL HAVE YOUR VERY OWN PRIVATE SWIMMING POOL.
ACE BUILDER

Developers and builders are well versed in the art of building close relationships with powerful and influential netas and babus. This allows them to build palatial homes, five-star hotels, exclusive resorts, glitzy malls and sprawling farm houses for the well-off, and earn enormous profits in the process. They rarely show any interest in projects that involve building housing facilities for the poor. There are cases where builders have surreptitiously altered building projects for the poor and built palatial apartments for the rich instead. Even housing laws are passed at their behest and their cosy relationship with the political class ensures protection from any punitive action.

THE REPORT SAYS THAT THE BUILDER HAS BEEN ACCUSED OF CHEATING, FRAUD AND POOR CONSTRUCTION. DO YOU THINK HE WILL APPEAR IN COURT?
NHA!! MORE LIKELY HE'LL APPEAR ON PAGE 3.

Despite it being six decades since Independence, countless citizens of this country still live in abysmal conditions, with no access to permanent shelter or basic utilities. Now and then one does read about ambitious schemes of the government and private companies to build urban housing for the poor, but in the end they just turn out to be a band-aid solution.

There is a lot of talk but little action to remove slums. Single-level pavement slums become double-storey structures and a cluster of shanties becomes a full-fledged colony. One almost gets the impression that there is an overriding ulterior, and perhaps sinister, motive for putting the brakes on slum eradication.

As long as the tide of migration from the villages to the cities is not stemmed, all efforts to provide decent housing will come to naught. It will remain a game of catch up. There is also a new trend of annexing surrounding villages to an existing city. It seems to be a profitable proposition for local politicians and their developer/builder buddies. These add-ons only worsen the infrastructure and administration of the city. Gandhiji, in his time, had advocated that villages should strive for self-reliance and self-sufficiency. He called it 'village swaraj'. Sadly, ever since Independence, villages have been ignored at the expense of cities. Maybe the time has come to revisit the concept of self-sufficiency of villages.

Perhaps, where feasible, clusters of villages near a large city can be integrated into independent mini-cities and developed by providing necessary utilities and infrastructure using locally available resources.

Agriculture, using innovative ideas and implements, should be primarily focussed on. Wherever possible, setting up of small-scale, labour-intensive industry using local products and resources can be encouraged to supplement the income of farmers during the lean season. Decent schools and colleges, adequate medical facilities and social services should be made available. The archaic system, dating back to the British era, of control radiating from the centre needs to be reviewed and a decentralised approach using modern administrative techniques can be incorporated for village administration.

It is only when villages attain self-sufficiency and are managed effectively using local authority and control, that the exodus from villages will cease and the urban crisis precipitated in cities, due to in-bound migration, come to an end.

When the uncontrolled and lopsided expansion of cities is contained, builders will have no choice but to look for work elsewhere. Maybe they will then relent and start paying attention to the needs of the *aam aadmi* instead of just catering to the rich. They need to be part of building a new India where there is a roof over the head of every citizen.

Whose Land Is It Anyway?

(Ode to the politician-developer-builder nexus)

This land is your land,
This land is my land,
From yonder hilltops,
To the spot where we stand;

From the distant valley;
To the lush green farmland;
And all the river banks,
And their stones and sand;

We have all approvals,
We have all titles,
We have all permissions,
Right here in our hand.

Wherever you look,
Whatever you see,
This vast open land;
Belongs to you and me.

(Inspired by a well-known American song)

Posters on the Wall

Politics and Public Education

A sizeable percentage of our children educated in the public school system are considered by employers as 'functionally illiterate'. Under-qualified and underpaid teachers, overcrowded and ill-equipped schools, poor policies and abysmal administration all contribute to this situation.

To top it all, petty regional political outfits, in the guise of regional pride, have ensured that children in municipal or village schools are educated only in their regional language. English is an anathema to these self-proclaimed and selfish netas. Don't they understand that a working knowledge of English is their only hope to become employable in better paying jobs? What is more galling is that these very netas send their own children to elite private English medium schools and colleges. Perhaps it is a deliberate attempt to keep the youth functionally illiterate. The young and unemployable males mutate into a kind of brainwashed militia who blindly follow the orders of their political masters. Educated people make choices, the uneducated follow directions. That is the mantra.

TEACHER! TEACHER! THEY'VE COME.
WHAT? THE FREE SWEATERS FOR THE COMING WINTER?
NO. THE FREE RAINCOATS THAT WERE TO BE DISTRIBUTED LAST MONSOON.
MUNICIPAL SCHOOL

MUNICIPAL SCHOOL
NETA-JI, YOU NEED TO PROVIDE TABLETS FOR ALL THE SCHOOL CHILDREN.
WHY? ARE THEY ALL SICK?

'Maths quiz. If a teacher's salary is ₹ 60,000 a year, and she has not been paid for 3 months ... how much money does the state owe her??'

Another development that is somewhat disturbing is that education has become a lucrative business for netas. Ever noticed how many educational institutes are owned or patronised by politicians? Trust them to diversify wherever money can be made, especially from the humongous capitation fees paid by the students during admissions. Education then is only available to the highest bidder. The weaker sections are left out in the cold. This educator-politician nexus is an alarming development that needs to controlled.

Some aspects of education did become a hot-button issue recently with the intervention of the Supreme Court and its directives on the RTE Act. We will need to wait and watch what comes out of all the hullabaloo it has generated.

RTE Act

'All private schools shall be required to enroll children from weaker sections and disadvantaged communities in their incoming class to the extent of 25% of their enrolment, by simple random selection. No seats in this quota can be left vacant. These children will be treated on par with all the other children in the school and subsidized by the State at the rate of average per learner costs in the government schools (unless the per learner costs in the private school are lower).'

(Right to Education Act, Source:—http://www.icbse.com/right-to-education-act)

RTE and Me

I was born in a small village in Kashmir in the early '40s. As was typical in those days, the village had no running water, no plumbing, no medical facilities, not even a decent school. I grew up blissfully unaware of what urban living was all about. The Second World War was raging and the British were desperately looking for Indians to make up for the shortage of English officers. My father was selected for commission as an officer in the Indian Army and sent overseas to fight the war. Life however, in our simple village continued uninterrupted.

In the mean time, the struggle for freedom was in full swing and Independence was achieved in 1947. Sadly, with Independence came the Partition of India and we were uprooted from our village and had to relocate to a big city in eastern India where my father was posted after the war. Imagine a six-year-old village urchin, with a rather primitive upbringing, suddenly thrust in an urban environment.

During the 'British Raj' there were boarding schools all over India that catered exclusively to the needs of British children. The average Indian was excluded from these elite schools. Post-Independence, these hoity-toity schools had no choice but to open their doors to all Indians. Perhaps one can term this development as the first 'Right to Education' in our country.

I spent a year as a boarder in one such 'elite' school, and believe me, from a village yokel who only knew his native tongue, who had never seen a tap or ever used a toilet, I was transformed into a mini 'Brown Sahib'. I began to speak fluent English, had impeccable manners, dressed in formal clothing and nowhere resembled the village bumpkin I once was. Attaining my full potential in the years to follow and becoming what I am today, was only possible because of the 'Right to Education' afforded me as a child six decades ago.

Yes. The current 'Right to Education' in private elite schools can work only if the underpriviledged children are afforded the opportunity for admission in boarding schools and their costly education is funded by the government.

The current RTE Act doesn't apply to boarding schools and as such, children according to this Act will be attending day schools only. My first concern is whether any study has been conducted of the psychological impact on the impressionable minds of these less fortunate children when they are allowed to experience the world of the privileged class for a few hours daily and that being over, to revert to their humble surroundings. We are a class-driven society and no amount of denial can alter that fact. The gap between the haves and have-nots is so enormous that I wonder if it can ever be bridged. So, the questions that arise are:

'What will a child think when a classmate arrives in a Mercedes or a BMW while they are dropped off on a cycle?

Will they get a free midday meal and will it look like the pizza, pasta, or parathas that their classmates will be eating?

After being exposed to the neatness of the school and its clean bathrooms, what will happen when they return home and have to make do with abysmal sanitary facilities in their slums or shanty towns?

Who will help them to do their homework, or monitor their progress?

What about sports? Who will provide them expensive sports gear or fancy school uniforms, shoes, stationery etc.?

Will classroom friendships that develop between children from different strata of society extend to home visits and interaction among parents?

How will they cope during the long vacations when they revert for an extended period to their unfortunate and undesirable surroundings? Will all that was learnt be lost?

What I fear most is that unscrupulous petty politicians and babus, will manipulate the system, obtain false certificates of income, caste etc. and usurp the quotas in elite schools. After all, they do it when there is housing to be allocated or ration cards to be issued, so what would stop them from misusing RTE?

I feel a better option for the central government would be to consider creating an extensive national network of schools primarily for underprivileged children patterned on the lines of the Kendriya Vidyalayas or the Sainik Schools. Why not provide every city, town, or cluster of villages with such special charter schools, the difference being that a larger percentage be reserved for the weaker sections of society? They could be called 'Bharatiya Vidyala'. Thus, not just the children that are proposed to be palmed off to private schools, but all children get education in a school setting in which they are socially comfortable. Let the excuse of paucity of funds not hoodwink the *aam aadmi* into believing it can't be done.

To me, the RTE Act appears to be an attempt by the government to wriggle out of its inability to provide decent education to underprivileged children and quietly shift the responsibility to private schools. It is just a token and misplaced measure that will achieve very little.

The implementation of RTE needs to be reviewed and every conceivable impact on the child thought through before forcing it on private schools. My plea to the powers that be—please don't short-change the deserving underprivileged kids.

Unless there is a parallel upliftment in the standard of living of the parents of those children who are supposed to benefit from RTE, I fear we may be doing a disservice to the children by exposing them to material desires that they can ill afford. Their innocent minds will not be able to comprehend the reasons.

Our poor children too are a precious asset. They too must be part of the future growth of our country. We must help them to succeed. But I don't think RTE is the way. They need to get an education in a comfortable environment not necessarily in an affluent one.

Help them but don't play politics with their education.

Dear Reader,

My views on RTE will, I'm sure, raise the hackles of many of you, especially the activists, and I will be branded as an elitist. Nothing can be further from the truth. I am not an elitist but a realist. Policies that look good on paper do not necessarily succeed when they are physically implemented on the ground. The impact of such policies on innocent children reared in an obnoxious but nevertheless rigid class/caste structure, that is the curse of our society, cannot be ignored and wished away.

All I am suggesting is that such considerations must be factored in when dreaming of welfare schemes meant to help the weaker sections of our society.

The focus of our leaders should be to, once and for all, abolish caste and do all it takes to narrow the wide gap between various sections of society. It will take time but it can be done. In the US, a janitor, (we would perhaps call him a sweeper) and the office boss may be far apart on the administrative chart of an organisation, but in the evening you may see them at the same bar having a drink together. Their children will, in all probability, be attending the same school too.

We, unfortunately, are nowhere near that stage yet.

Who's In Charge?

India's Youth Brigade

'Hum laye hain toofan se kashti ko nikal ke;
Is desh ko rakhna bachchon sambhal ke.'

(We have steered the boat out of the storm;
O children of this country please keep it safe now)

This patriotic song sung by the late Mohammad Rafi pretty much sums up what the great leaders of yesteryear expected of the younger generations. Is the current youth, that constitutes almost thirty per cent of the population, up to taking on the task that will eventually be entrusted to them? Are they worried about or actively involved in the fight against poor governance, and rampant corruption that is afflicting the country today? Sadly, in the past few years, other than a fizzled-out recent protest against corruption and a short-lived agitation for women's rights, I haven't seen any sustained national movement spearheaded by the youth that has challenged the establishment.

Soon, the steering wheel of the country will be in their hands. Should they not become aware of the dangers they are likely to confront when it's their turn to navigate the turbulent and treacherous waters of flawed politics and poor governance? Is it also not their responsibility to figure out how they will chart a course that leads the country to the calmer waters of progress and prosperity for all its citizens?

What?
Us?
Worry?

(*Inspired by Alfred E. Neuman—'What, Me Worry?'*)

The Indian youth is a diverse lot. There are the affluent ones who often make the news when they mow down innocent people while driving their BMWs in an inebriated state or get into bar fights that often end with someone getting shot. They are least bothered about their country.

Then there are youths who join the military/paramilitary forces or work for big private companies. They are generally well provided for and are not directly affected by issues that affect the common man.

A growing section comprises of college students and 'back office' employees, who are generally in the news when they get arrested at rave parties. Their preoccupation after work is searching for a new watering hole, the next rock concert, or the new gig in town. They can be often seen driving dangerously and flouting all traffic rules. Barring a few, they have no time or inclination to get involved in whatever ails the country.

Some people think rules and signs,
Are really just a token;
It's no big deal, if occasionally,
Some of them are broken.

Lastly, there is the functionally illiterate, unemployable and disgruntled youth, mostly migrants from villages. A pathetic public education system deprived them of the knowledge and skills needed for survival in today's world. Some find work in the service industry or as a domestic help. Others join crime syndicates or become the lackeys of petty political outfits and can be seen vandalising property, setting buses on fire, and generally creating mayhem in offices, cinema theatres, or on the street whenever a self-proclaimed local neta wants to create a politically motivated disturbance.

The youth is our future and by remaining on the sidelines, they are doing a disservice to the nation. Perhaps a charismatic messiah is needed to shake them out of their complaisant attitude and inspire them to become more politically and socially conscious and get involved in the burning issues of the day. They must collectively challenge the establishment if they perceive that the geriatric leadership is out of touch with their future aspirations. They must become the instrument of change and strive to make a difference in the country.

Let them start by taking a cue from US President Obama's 2008 election slogan, and commit to the nation, in a loud and clear voice:

'Yes we can. Yes we will.'

If they don't, their indifference is tantamount to aiding and abetting those who have snatched our country from us.

SO WHEN YOU AND THE OTHER STUDENTS GHERAOED THE NETA AND DEMANDED CHANGE, WHAT DID HE DO?
HE GAVE ME A HANDFUL OF COINS.
WE WANT CHANGE

I'M WORRIED BECAUSE
I DON'T SEE ANY SIGN OF THEM
BEING WORRIED.
TONIGHT
ROCK
CONCERT

Words for teenagers

(Words spoken by an American judge who regularly deals with the youth.)

'The world does not owe you a living, you owe the world something. You owe it your time, energy and talent … grow up, stop being a crybaby, get out of your dream world and develop a backbone not a wishbone. Start behaving like a responsible person. You are important and you are needed. It's too late to sit around and wait for somebody to do something someday. Someday is now and that somebody is you!

(Source: *http://www.huffingtonpost.com/2012/08/14/words-for-teenagers-judge-advice_n_1776337.html*)

Recently, a section of the student population and some enlightened youths actively demonstrated their outrage and resolved to fight fearlessly for a cause that affected their well-being and safety. One can only hope this new awakening is not just a transient phenomenon and that the youth will have the stamina to sustain the momentum and fight for other important causes too in the days ahead.

Most of the youth is tech-savvy and they have used the social media to mobilise collective protests on issues that are important to them. Social media is a powerful tool and no doubt is giving the establishment sleepless nights. I'm sure a 'dirty tricks' department somewhere in the administration is figuring out ways to curb its effectiveness. All the more reason for the youth to remain vigilant.

It seems that this awakening so far is confined to urban areas, and that too, in larger cities. It needs to spread to all corners of the country. Every citizen needs to introspect and question why even after six decades of Independence we still have poverty, lawlessness, a degraded environment, and a sense of deprivation. They should demand change. Only then can the collective voice of the people make any impact and only then will we truly be able to call ourselves a functional democracy.

Pollution Vollution Ka Kya Solution?

Whether it is visuals on TV of garbage choking the streets of our cities or filth flowing into the sacred Ganga, it is clear that in this country the environment is under attack from within.

Industries don't care if effluents flow into rivers or poisonous gases are released from chimneys. Municipalities don't care if sewage flows into streams or garbage rots on the roadside. Developers don't care if their projects are the cause of the vanishing green cover. People don't care if they litter, spit or defecate wherever they please. We, as a nation, have a long way to go before consciousness about the environment is ingrained in our psyche. Only by being sensitive and aware can we prevent the degradation of our environment.

To expand on a quote of Walt Kelly, (creator of Pogo)—in the war to preserve the environment, we have seen the enemy, and it is us.

It is a matter of national shame that a recent survey showed that there are more cell phones in the country than toilets. Verbal connectivity appears to have triumphed over basic sanitary facilities. Perhaps the intention is to go to the fields and give back to Mother Nature the product that resulted from eating the bountiful harvest she provided in the first place. But, with the alarming increase in population, we shouldn't overload her!

A neta, some time ago, said that India requires more toilets than it does more temples. This created such an uproar as though he had said something sacrilegious. It only shows the indifference of the common man towards adopting a hygienic and non-polluting way of performing morning ablutions.

There are states that have made it compulsory for anyone who is a candidate in the local elections, to show proof of having an attached toilet in their dwelling.

Do we have such low-level criteria to ascertain suitability of our leaders of tomorrow?

Of Pots and Plans

Many years ago, I was involved as an illustrator, in a government scheme to promote toilets in villages. They needed posters that would, through graphic images, motivate village folk to use toilets that were specially designed using materials available locally. The scheme was well conceived and should have achieved what it was planned for, but it had not factored in the stubborn resistance by the rural folk to break their daily traditional need for early morning communion with nature. No amount of visual or oral persuasion seemed to have had any significant impact. I was told that the villagers found another use for the stand-alone toilets. They were an excellent storage facility.

I'm sure, conscientious planners and social scientists are back at their drawing boards trying to devise other schemes. I can only wish them well.

THE SILENT SCREAM !

Be it the train driver with a sadistic streak tooting the engine horn at 2 am, or the stone-deaf DJ pumping up the music volume to high decibel levels at about the same time, or the marriage parties that cannot do without 'BOOMs' and 'BANGs' at unearthly hours, or the canine species wanting to settle territorial disputes at midnight—we are constantly assaulted by unwanted sounds that deprive all of us of a good night's rest. It appears that it's a culture in India to celebrate by generating noise.

Despite strict guidelines laid down by the Supreme Court on noise levels, none of the agencies who need to monitor and take action on violations seem to show any interest in reducing noise pollution. This despite medical evidence of the harmful effects it has on the well-being of humans. It is left to concerned activists to fight, what seems to be a losing battle in curbing this menace.

The Sound of Silence

After having spent 20 years in a small suburb of Boston, USA, the most difficult adjustment on my return to India, was getting used to the increased decibel levels. In the vicinity of where I now live, is a bar/lounge/restaurant/ that is a sort of watering hole for the nocturnal party animals of the city. It plays loud music in an outdoor setting, well beyond the legally permissible time and decibel limits, sometimes well into the wee hours of the morning.

Even with the windows shut, the noise of the techno music makes it impossible for one to sleep. Calls to the police result in a cop coming to the joint and directing the owners to lower the volume. However, as soon as they leave, the volume is cranked up again. Sometime back, I addressed a letter to the collector, who is supposed to be the head of a committee that is entrusted with ensuring compliance with the Supreme Court directive on noise. He in turn passed it on to the Municipal Corporation, that in turn passed it on to the Pollution Control Board and since I never got a reply, perhaps it was passed on to the office peon, who conveniently crumpled it and threw it in the waste paper basket. End of story.

One night, celebrations including loud music and bursting of firecrackers in an open-air marriage hall in the neighbourhood, continued well past midnight. I called the police helpline to have them shut down the festivities. The cop who responded to my call, gave me a gem of a reply. 'C'mon, give them a break. So what if it's continuing past the legal time limit? How can we play spoilsport on such an auspicious occasion!'

On another occasion, regarding a similar matter I called the city Pollution Control Department and requested them to send someone to do some measurements so that I could file a police complaint. The reply I got was—'Sorry. At the moment, we don't have any functioning decibel meters.'

Maybe I need to get a pair of ear plugs or else invest in expensive Fenesta windows, in order to sleep at night.

Other than casually littering every inch of free space around us, we are also a nation of compulsive chewers and spitters. We love our paan, *supari*, gutkha, and tobacco. Walk anywhere and you are bound to see telltale signs of someone having consumed, masticated, and orally expelled some icky-coloured blob that has left its mark on roads, sidewalks, boundary walls or corners of staircases.

Chewing and spitting, apart from being a filthy and unhygienic habit, leaves stains that are an ugly sight. Most of the products chewed are known carcinogens. Sadly, no one really cares what these careless habits do to the environment. Recently, a ban was imposed on use of plastic and also on the sale and consumption of gutkha. As with all bans, it has hardly made any difference.

'Yes. Jogging outdoors sure helped me with my wieght problem, but now... Cough!! Cough!! Wheeze!!... thanks to the air outside, I have a lung problem.'

In India, the weaker sections of society are least bothered about air pollution. They, in their daily struggle for existence, use anything that can burn to help them cook their frugal meals, regardless of the consequences of doing so. A belly full of food is more important than lungs full of clean air.

In urban areas, sporadic measures to tackle air pollution have been taken from time to time, but with the proliferation of cars and two-wheelers on the roads, it appears to be a losing proposition. In rural settings, in an effort to limit the burning of firewood, the use of biogas and solar heating has been experimented with. Much more needs to be done.

Air pollution and its impact on health is a critical issue and cannot be brushed aside. I read somewhere that polluted air reduces one's lifespan by nine years. It is therefore important that all government agencies get their act together and work towards taking practical measures to tackle this issue. They should take lessons from European countries, where vehicles are restricted from entering major cities; using public transport, cycles and carpooling is encouraged while production of petrol-guzzling luxury cars is discouraged. But that's asking too much, both of the government and also the people.

So, in typical Indian fashion, let us all resign ourselves to Fate and continue to inhale polluted air with every breath we take.

Last but not the least, there is water pollution. There is a need to ... Oh!! Forget it. The less said, the better.

Doggy Doo

DID YOU SEE THAT?
HE PICKED UP AFTER HIS DOG.
MUST BE AN NRI.*
KEEP
YOUR CITY
CLEAN
*Non Resident Indian

Random Reflections

A Collection of Prose, Poetry, and Parody

All Indians are equal … but some Indians are more equal than others

(Modified maxim inspired by George Orwell's *Animal Farm*.)

*Perhaps the neta thought OBE (acronym for Order of the British Empire) stood for Other Backward Englishmen.

Jokes aside, the biggest disservice the political class has done to the *aam aadmi* in the six decades since Independence, is tacitly supporting the perpetuation of the inequalities inherent in the caste/class system, broadly identified by their abbreviated forms SC, ST and OBC. It appears there is a kind of vested interest or maybe even a sinister political objective to ensure that this caste/class based classification and special/preferential entitlements endure. This has resulted in a ridiculous situation that all manner of people clamour to get lower caste/class certificates, legally or illegally, just to qualify for these special benefits.

Just before the elections, regional politicians seek votes from specific caste/class vote banks. Government employment and even promotions will perhaps have percentages set aside based on caste/class. These are measures that go against the equal rights guaranteed under the constitution for every citizen.

What is needed is a cultural revolution of sorts to change the mindset of the leaders and citizens of our country that ensures all Indians accept each other as 'Equal Citizens' in every sense of the words.

Caste/class has no place in modern India.

(Quote- http://en.wikipedia.org/wiki/Animal_Farm
'All animals are equal, but some animals are more equal than others.')

Peek-a-boo!!

Political leaders must strive for an image makeover so that the title neta, is not considered a mere four letter word.

If

If you can meet politicians and crooks,
And discover some are one and the same;
Yet go out and vote and let them win,
'cause elections are only a game.

If you can meet inefficiency and corruption,
And find ways to survive the same,
And accept that there is no way out
'cause you don't know whom to blame.

If you accept most netas are goons,
And lazy babus are always on a break,
And no one cares a hoot about the law,
'cause the police too are on the take.

If you can sidestep roadside garbage,
Or avoid falling in an uncovered drain,
Or zigzag your way through unending traffic,
Without someone snatching your chain.

If smelly public toilets don't sicken you,
And you're accustomed to garbage stench.
And diesel fumes don't bother you,
While sitting on a bus-stop bench.

If you think greasing of palms is OK,
'cause that's how things are done.
And your attitude is 'Chalta Hai'
'cause it's the same as everyone.

If nothing around you upsets you,
And you feel that 'Aal eez well',
Then you're a true Indian my friend,
I truly wish you well.

(Inspired by Rudyard Kipling's poem)

I had a nightmare

(Inspired by Martin Luther King's 'I have a dream' speech.)

I had a nightmare that the people of this country had turned into zombies, who shuffled around in response to harsh commands barked at them by hordes of crooks and goons who had seized the reins of power at all levels of governance in the country.

I had a nightmare that the scary images conjured up in George Orwell's *1984* were for real. There was a newly created Ministry of Persecution that went after any zombie, who, through any word or deed, threatened or stood up to the goons in power.

I had a nightmare that there was a Ministry of Morality whose guiding principle was—'do as I say' and not 'do as I do'. This allowed crooks in power to loot the country or rape its zombies without fear of any retribution.

I had a nightmare that the majestic mountains stood naked, denuded of all trees. The mighty rivers had become open filthy drains and the pristine lush green valleys had become stinking garbage dumps.

I had a nightmare that the birds in the air, the wild animals in the forests, and the fishes in the lakes and seas had fled the country and its shores, to take refuge elsewhere in safer surroundings.

I had a nightmare that the country went bankrupt because with so many crooks in power, all the wealth of the country had been siphoned off and stashed away in foreign banks.

I had a nightmare that inflation had gone through the roof rendering the currency so worthless that the zombies were using currency notes to light fires for cooking.

The last image of my nightmare was that of a long line of zombie citizens, including me, shuffling along, and moving towards a distant well. One by one, they jumped into the well and disappeared. It was the well of despair.

I too jumped in ... that's when I woke up with a start.

Was it really a nightmare?

Are we those zombies?

Ye Desh hain tera aur mera

(Inspired by a popular American song-'This Land is your Land')

Ye desh hain tera,
Ye desh hain mera,
Himalay ki chotiyon se,
Kanya-kumari tak:
Paschim ke reton se,
Purav ke kheton tak,
Ye desh hain tera aur mera.

Aao sab mil kar,
Garibi hatayen,
Is desh me se,
Bhukh mitayen;
Aao hum dekhen,
Ek naya save-e–ra,
Yeh desh hain tera aur mera.

Himmat badayain,
Insaaf ko payain,
Aaman aur shanti,
Ko hum apnayain,
Sab logo mein,
Pyaar baantein,
Aur hatay-ain bhrashtachar.

Bharat mahan tha,
Duniya ki shaan tha,
Vapas banana,
Hamara kaam hain;
Hath mila kar,
Awaaz uthaa kar,
Aao ye mil ke ga-yain.

Ye desh hain tera,
Ye desh hain mera,
Himalay ki chotiyon se,
Kanya-kumari tak;
Paschim ke reton se,
Purav ke kheton tak,
Ye desh hain tera aur mera;

Ye desh hain tera aur mera;

Ye desh hain tera … aur … meraa

English translation

This is your country,
This is my country,
From the Himalayas,
To Kanya-kumari:
From the western deserts,
To the fields in the east,
This country belongs to you and me.

Let's come together,
And remove poverty,
And also hunger,
From the country:
Come let's look for,
A new dawn,
This country is yours and mine.

Let's have the courage,
And demand justice,
And adopt the path
Of goodwill and peace;
And spread the message of love,
Among all people,
And remove corruption.

India was a great country,
Had a glorious place in the world,
Returning it to that glory,
Is now our task;
Let's join hands,
And raise our voice
And sing together;

This is your country,
This is my country,
From the Himalayas,
To Kanya-kumari:
From the western deserts,
To the fields in the east,
This country belongs to you and me.

This country belongs to you and me.

This country belongs to you and me.

Pomp, Pageantry, and Perplexity

Article 53(1) of the Constitution vests in the President "[t]he executive power of the Union", to be "exercised by him [sic] either directly or through officers subordinate to him" in accordance with the provisions of the Constitution. However, the Constitution also states that the Council of Ministers, headed by the Prime Minister, is "to aid and advise the President who shall, in the exercise of his functions, act in accordance with such advice".

An awful lot of tax payers' money is spent on maintaining the residence of a person whom some consider to be a ceremonial figurehead, and whose responsibility and accountability under the constitution is somewhat nebulous. I'm no constitutional expert so I'm naturally a bit confused.

If the ultimate political authority lies elsewhere and not with the resident of Rashtrapati Bhavan, an idle thought arises—why do we need a President? Of course, no politician in his or her right mind will ever raise this issue, perhaps they too must secretly be aspiring to move into that grand relic of British colonial times. So, if that be so, perhaps we should try to figure out ways to lessen the burden on tax-paying citizens. For that, why not make money out of Presidentship? Make all the pomp and show that goes on in Rashtrapati Bhavan a spectacle for tourists and the public on a daily basis. Parading the Presidential bodyguards, in their bright and colourful uniforms, mounted on magnificent horses, will be a sure money spinner. Regular tours of the palace and gardens at a price can also rake in money. Souvenirs of miniature statues of the uniformed guards, the palace, plaques/portraits of the current resident and a host of other knick-knacks can be marketed at the premises. Special banquets can be hosted, where those with moolah can have a grand meal and get pictures taken with the resident, all for a tidy donation to the upkeep fund. Marriages of family members of the occupant can be conducted in the palace and televised by channels that make the highest bid. The possibilities are endless.

Any takers?

(In what is surely a remarkable coincidence, my thoughts about making Rashtrapati Bhavan a money-spinner, conjured up many months ago, appear to have been telepathically transmitted to the Presidential entourage. Parading of the Presidential Guard for the entertainment of the aam aadmi, and also charging a nominal fee for a tour of the buildings and gardens of the Rashtrapati Bhahavan, have recently been reported in the media.)

2014. Who will occupy this hot seat?

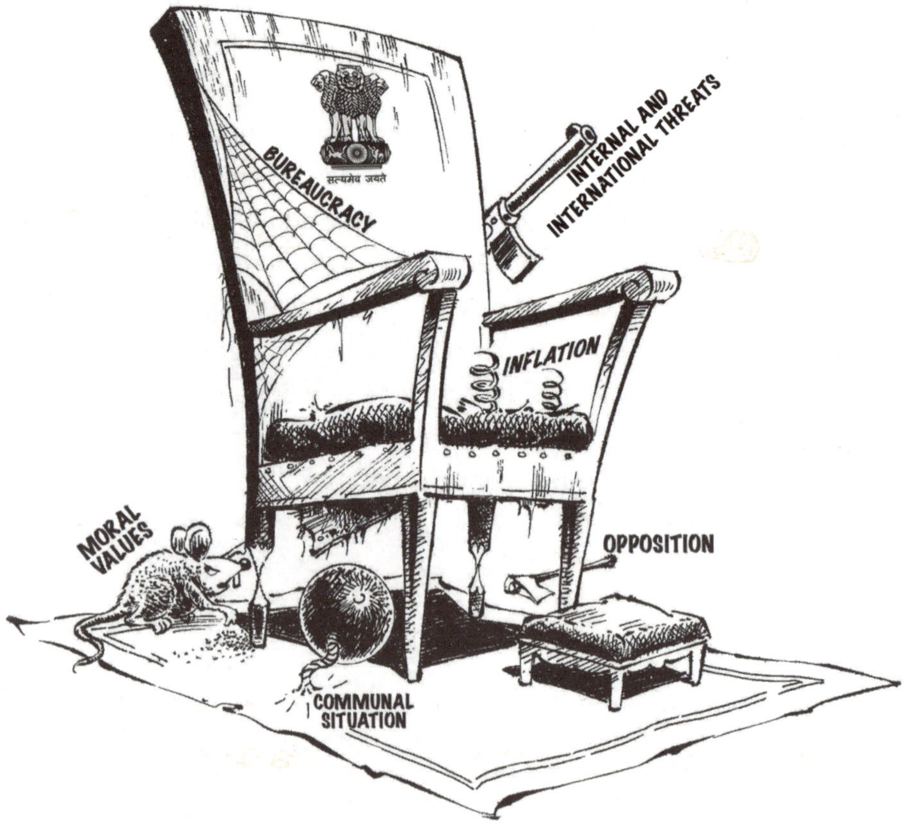

Bombay, Mumbai, whatever!

I left the beautiful and vibrant city of Bombay in 1985 for an extended stay in the US for twenty years. When I returned in 2005, the city had vanished. I landed in a city called Mumbai. Good grief, what happened to my beloved city Bombay?

Preliminary enquiries revealed that some political outfit suddenly discovered that the name 'Bombay' was a legacy of colonial British rule and an affront to the sensibilities of a free India. I pondered on the logic used in this name change and wondered what else would follow. Would there be a demand to rip out all the rail tracks laid by the British? Would there be a clamour to use a wrecking ball and flatten the Gateway of India?

Well the deed has been done. Bombay has officially morphed into Mumbai. But if our nation can have multiple names, India and Bharat, why can't my beloved city too have two equally valid names, Bombay and Mumbai?

Keep your Mumbai, but I want my Bombay back.
(And also Calcutta, Madras, Poona, Baroda, Bangalore, Pondicherry etc.)

Running Scared

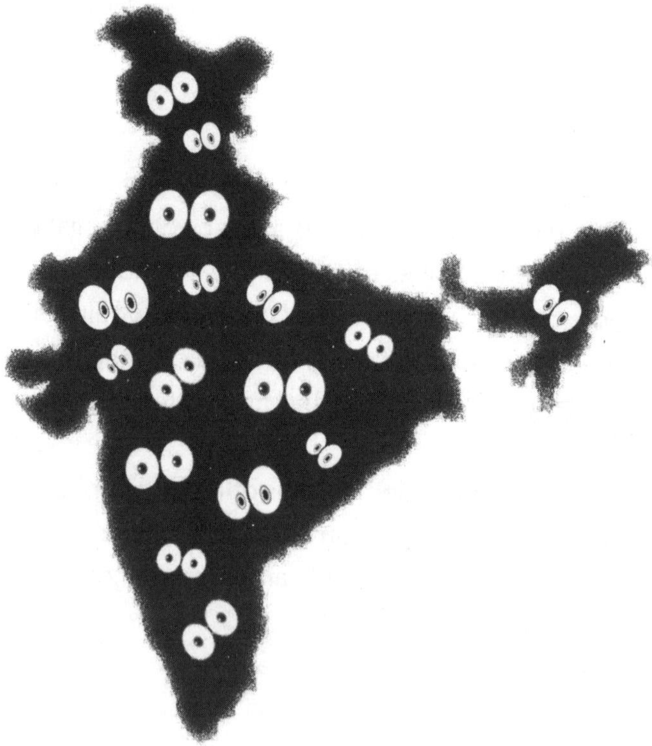

We are a nation of scared people. Members of the political class, babus, military and paramilitary forces, etc. are scared of RTI activists and whistle-blowers. RTI activists and whistle-blowers are scared that powerful politicians or businessmen will snuff them out. The media executives are scared they will be harassed if they expose the nefarious activities of the powerful.

The business community is scared of raids by the Income Tax department. The Income Tax department is scared that some of their own shenanigans will be discovered. Bollywood is scared of radical groups and gangsters. Gangsters are scared they'll be eliminated by their rivals. Lovers are scared of the Khaps. Late night revellers at discos and clubs are scared they'll be rounded up and booked. Wives are scared of abusive husbands. Young girls are scared they'll be molested. Children are scared of sadistic teachers. Teachers are scared they won't get their salaries on time. The high and mighty at all levels are scared that their holier-than-thou image will be defaced by cartoons, caricatures and YouTube spoofs. Cartoonists and creative artists are scared they will be imprisoned on sedition charges. People making innocent comments on the social media are scared they will be arrested by the police. The scared police buckles under political pressure. Netas are scared they will be slapped or booed if they dare interact with the man on the street.

There are many other people who are scared for many other reasons, but what scares the majority of Indians the most is the direction in which this country is heading.

We Too Are to Blame

The year was 1956. I was a teenager visiting Bangalore for the first time. It was a clean, beautiful city then, unlike what it is today, a filthy, concrete jungle. I was taking a stroll in the evening along MG Road, taking in the sights and sounds of the city. Those days there were hardly any cars, so most people were either walking or on their bicycles. Soon, the sun set and it grew dark. Then it happened. Every single cyclist, must have been hundreds, dismounted from their bikes, took out a match box, lit the oil headlamp fixed in front of the handlebar, mounted and cycled on. What a wonderful demonstration of civic responsibility, respect for the law and self-discipline!

That image is etched in my memory. Those stellar qualities citizens had then are, alas, no longer in fashion. We no longer care to abide by the rules that need to be followed in a civilised society.

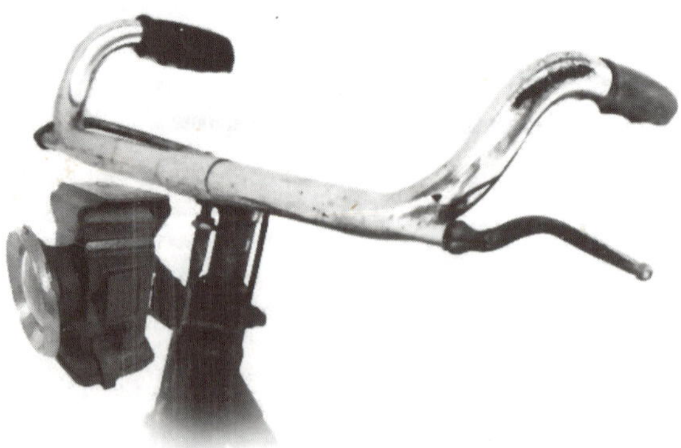

Something Fishy

'Give me a fish and I eat for a day. Teach me to fish and I eat for a lifetime.'

—Chinese proverb

I have often wondered why the wisdom of this saying has not found favour with the ruling class in India. Why is it that successive governments, whether at the centre or the states, keep giving the poor their daily dose of fish, yet don't empower them to fish on their own? They know that periodic grandiose schemes announcing handouts, such as various subsidies, TV sets, bicycles, laptops and now even direct transfer of cash to their bank accounts, hasn't translated into any tangible upliftment of the poor, who are mainly unemployed or else employed in the unorganised sector.

What is the compulsion to give sops that don't do much to alleviate poverty? Is the whole exercise a deep-rooted conspiracy, woven by the political class, to siphon off money? Are they ensuring that even with the meagre benefit amount that does reach them, the poor remain dependent and thus beholden to them for their magnanimity? Is this being done with the ulterior motive that the poor will remember them at election time, when truckloads of these economically captive poor folks are taken to voting booths to cast votes in favour of their perceived benefactors?

What I fail to understand is how can their conscience allow these failed schemes to continue. They know that the huge wasteful expenditure on these schemes only drives up the deficit that in turn results in inflation, which brings down the living standards of the middle class and causes untold grief to the poor. These schemes need to be discontinued, as the only people benefiting from them are those corrupt people who promote them.

To minimise poverty in a phased manner, there needs to be a vision of where we want all the citizens of this great country to be a decade from now. As a first step, the middle class must be allowed to prosper. They in turn can then pass on some of their increased income, by increasing salaries and benefits, to their employees, be it in farming, business or domestic employment. This gradual trickle-down improvement in the standard of living of the weaker section of our population will be quicker than from any top-down grandiose government measure.

The role of the government should be that of a facilitator. It must establish, in consultation with leading experts, what the realistic minimum wages and benefits for all citizens in the unorganised sector should be. It must focus on providing good schools, decent accommodation, basic infrastructure and utilities that are affordable and accessible to the weaker sections. To do this, it must ensure that the entrenched and corrupt nexus between politicians, developers and bureaucrats that has hindered and created obstacles, is shattered once and for all.

With these improvements in place, the people from the weaker sections of society will then be able to afford better and more useful education, proper nutrition and health coverage for their children. Armed with meaningful education and marketable skills, this generation of children can then aspire to attain a better standard of living and come out of the poverty cycle. These children would have then learnt how to 'fish'.

I have a dream that in the not-so-distant future, the scourge of poverty will disappear from India. It won't happen overnight, but it can happen if a charismatic, honest, enlightened, pragmatic and bold national leader emerges who has the courage to confront and overcome entrenched vested interests and do whatever it takes to rid the country of poverty. If such a leader does not emerge, eradication of poverty will sadly remain, just a pipe dream.

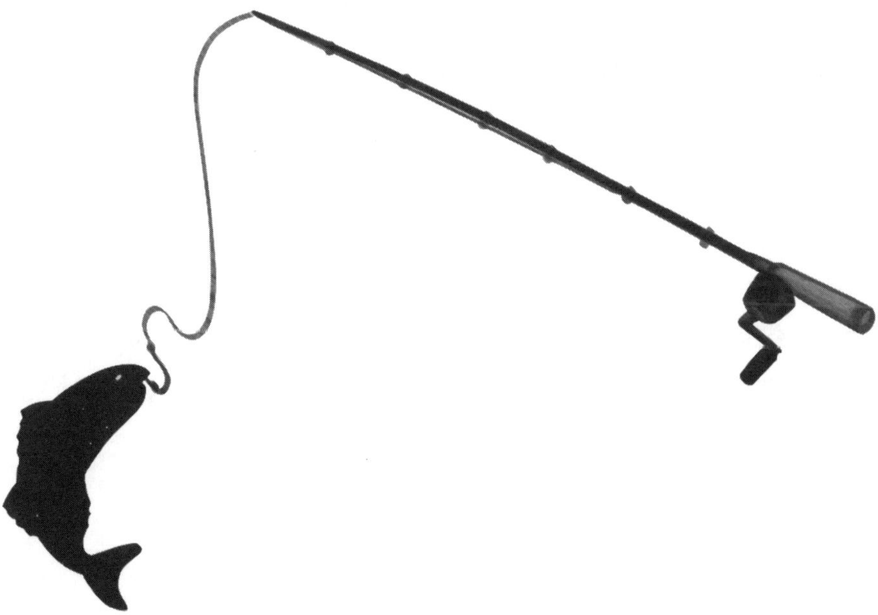

Activists, for whatever cause, are the watchdogs of the nation, who, without expectations of a material reward, commit themselves to protect the interests of the **aam aadmi.** *Their vigilance is what helps to keep a check on the ruling class if they show any tendency to blatantly misuse their power.*

However, the activists need to guard themselves from becoming so myopic in their cause, that they lose sight of the big picture.

Sorry. Not in My Backyard.

During the run-up to the last general elections, I met a retired bureaucrat, with exemplary credentials, who had floated a new party and was all set to contest in the elections. His pro-people and anti-corruption platform should have been an ideal message for the public. I asked him if he had tapped the voting potential of the large student population in colleges and universities, a section that would surely support such a party.

What he told me was an eye-opener, and a very disturbing one for a supposedly democratic country. It seems that most of these institutions are either owned by politicians or enjoy their patronage and protection. The funds ploughed into, or generated from them, are from questionable sources and a tight lid is kept on their functioning. They deny access to any activist or new political leader who might plant radical views in the minds of the students and uncover for them the real truth behind these institutions.

That perhaps explains the lack of any large scale student involvement in the politics of the country in past few decades.

'We Are Not Amused'

(This pretty much sums up the reaction of some politicians to cartoons and spoofs that have appeared in the electronic media and in textbooks.)

Like the Indian tiger—cartoonists in India have become a sort of endangered species. The difference being that the powers that be have no interest in preserving the species. The writing on the wall is, 'Don't mock the establishment or else ….'. This spells trouble. In a mature democracy, this form of intimidation by some members of the political class is a violation of the freedom of speech enshrined in our constitution.

I agree that cartoonists have to practise self-regulation to ensure that they desist from deliberately projecting a derogatory image of a specific individual, community or ethnic group, through innuendo or suggestive drawings in their cartoons. This *laxmanrekha* (deciding where to draw the line) is especially important in case of cartoonists who are also activists. They need to exercise judicious restraint in their graphics. On the flip side, our politicians need to be more mature in their reaction to a specific cartoon, especially if the object was to highlight an issue that is controversial and can be interpreted and viewed differently by the vast multitudes that call India their home.

It appears that the political class is getting a bit restless and uneasy with the negative image the public has of them. Their knee-jerk reaction every time a controversial cartoon makes news is symptomatic of an inner insecurity and a paranoia of anything that will deflate their ego. Often these netas occupy positions of power knowing that they do not have the qualifications or required credentials. They know deep down that they have failed the nation. They have failed to resist the evil and powerful forces of ego and greed. They are men of straw with feet of clay.

Only exemplary leadership, honesty, and integrity can earn them the respect and admiration of the man on the street. So, if they wish not to be lampooned by cartoonists, they should reform themselves and learn what it takes to be a leader. For a start, perhaps they should do a serious reading of the Bhagwad Gita and imbibe the knowledge and wisdom that is as relevant today as was centuries ago. They should get off their high horses and go beyond their circle of armed guards and interact with the common man. But wait a minute. If that happens, we cartoonists will be out of jobs. How can you poke fun at a neta who becomes so righteous that you can almost picture a halo around his head?

My guess is that it won't happen any time soon. So dear cartoonists, keep the ideas churning, the pens drawing, and give the country your take on events, creatively and fearlessly. This special species has to survive for the good of the country and preservation of democracy.

The Great Indian
Slideshow

Health of the Nation

Food for Thought

Payback Time

Spot the Leader

'No silly. The smart fellow in front is only a bodyguard. The leader is the little guy behind him.'

Power Play

DO YOU HAVE POWER IN THIS VILLAGE?
NO. THERE IS NO PAWAR. BUT WE DO HAVE A KAMBLE AND A SHINDE.

Pavement Dweller

Seeing Red

THERE GOES THE POMPOUS SARPANCH FLAUNTING HIS RED GLASS LANTERN.

Going to Pot

'YOU SEE DEAR, ONCE THE REMAINING BITS OF THE ROAD BECOME POTHOLES TOO, THE SURFACE WILL BE LEVEL AGAIN.'

Jam-Boree

YES DEAR! I'M STUCK IN TRAFFIC. NO, NOT CARS, BUSES OR TRUCKS ... COWS, BUFFALOES AND ELEPHANTS.

Clean Sweep

HE SAYS HE OVERHEARD YOU WANTING TO HAVE SOME SCAMS SWEPT UNDER THE CARPET.
CBI REPORT

Dig We Must

'Hurry up and repair that patch. I have to dig and lay a pipe there.'

Boxed In

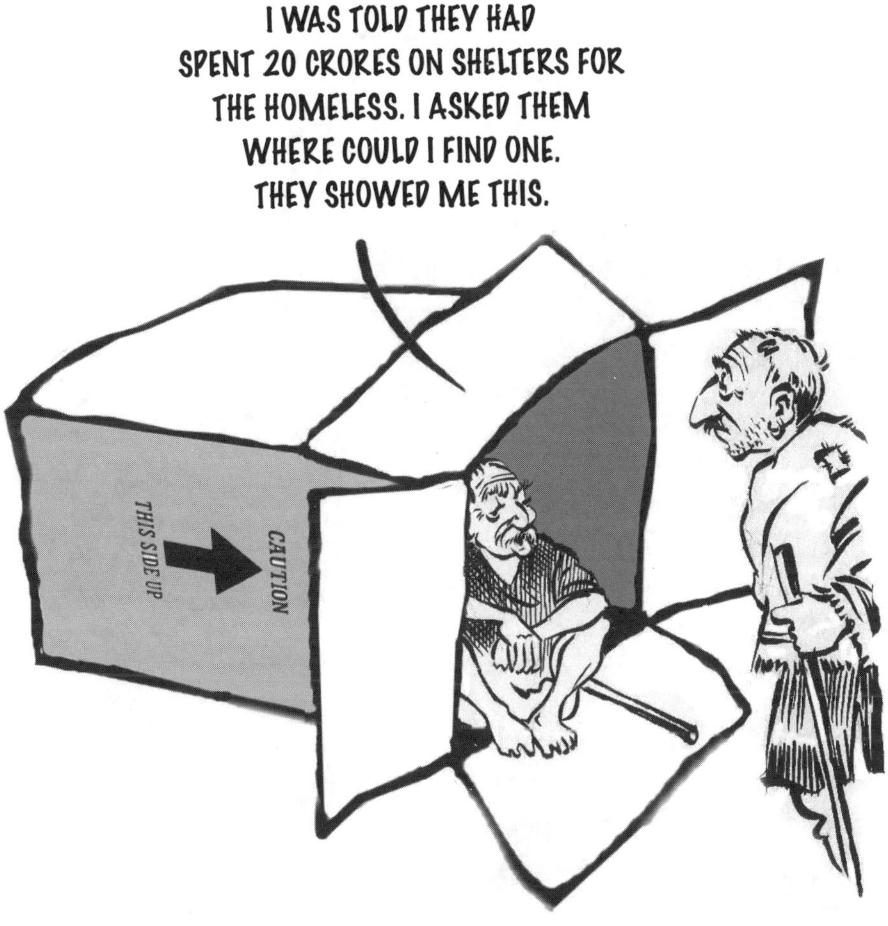
I WAS TOLD THEY HAD
SPENT 20 CRORES ON SHELTERS FOR
THE HOMELESS. I ASKED THEM
WHERE COULD I FIND ONE.
THEY SHOWED ME THIS.
CAUTION
THIS SIDE UP

Struggle for Existence

Car-Toon

SIR, I KNOW THAT WITH A FLASHING 'LAL BATTI' WE DON'T HAVE TO FOLLOW TRAFFIC RULES. BUT WE HAVE TO STOP. IT'S A ZEBRA CROSSING.
NONSENSE! KEEP GOING. I DON'T SEE ANY ZEBRAS CROSSING.

Care-Less Talk

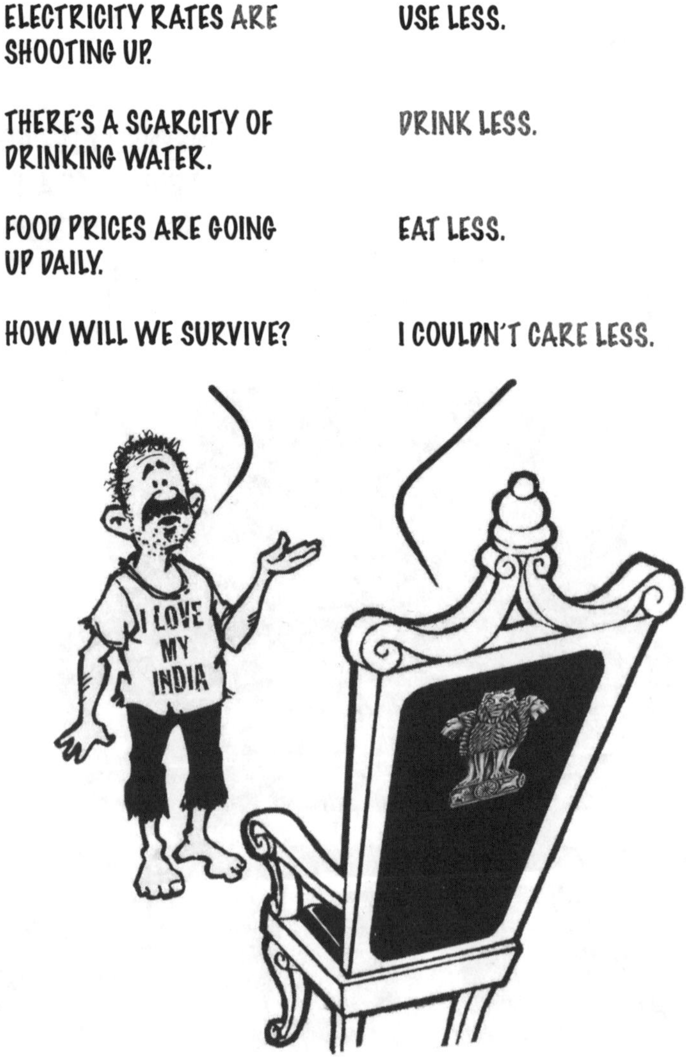

Whither Now?

I have often asked myself this question. Why has the *aam aadmi,* except on a few recent occasions, shown very little signs of any sustained or collective anger against bad and corrupt governance that is being exposed by the media, almost on a daily basis? Reaction appears to find vocal expression only in hyperventilating TV anchors, pontificating columnists, agitated social workers or angry activists.

One could perhaps explain it by quoting that Indians, by and large, stoically accept their destined fate. Not so, I found. In the urban setting the hard-working and sincere *aam aadmi* has too much at stake. They cannot take time off to join any form of mass protest against the unfair system that is heavily stacked against them. They cannot afford to lose their job and livelihood. They may be bitter, but they can't afford to be angry.

In rural areas, a nefarious nexus between the babu and the panchayat (which is conveniently comprised of mostly the family members of the sarpanch) ensures that the development funds flow into the pockets of these officials and a pittance is distributed to the villagers. Methods such as intimidation and coercion are used to stifle any opposition from the simple villagers. Fear is used to ensure that their anger remains suppressed and there is never a possibility for a collective rebellion.

So, the *aam aadmi* in urban India cannot afford to be angry and the *aam aadmi* in rural India is afraid to be angry.

A Ray of Sunshine

Amidst the doom and gloom and air of despair that pervades our dysfunctional democracy, one does see rays of sunshine and pockets of hope. There are dedicated individuals, social groups, and NGOs that are trying, in their own humble way, to fill in the void in areas where the government has failed its citizens.

One hears of the dedicated person in Bihar who seeks out intelligent village kids and successfully prepares them for admission to premier technology institutes. I know of a social group that runs an orphanage for educating girls and when they are ready for marriage, they provide for a simple wedding and give the girls utensils, bedding, and a stove—a sort of starter kit to set up a home.

There is a long list of NGOs that are doing a marvellous job in cities and villages by supplementing government programs that benefit the urban and rural communities. Some have programmes where socially-conscious college graduates and young professionals take time off from their jobs and commit to spend two years teaching in under-resourced municipal or village schools. Their focus is to give underprivileged children a strong educational foundation.

There are other centres that help rehabilitate the handicapped, or victims of child or spousal abuse, or drug addicts. Their only desire is to see a happy smile on the faces of people whose lives they have touched. The dedication of these people and groups needs to be applauded.

A large section of our marginalised population needs to be a part of the inclusive growth that elected officials keep promising. Individual volunteers and social groups can only do so much. They can only show, on a smaller scale, how help can be given. It is for the people in charge of governance to learn from them, formulate, fund, and execute practical national policies that will help uplift the downtrodden.

The government cannot abdicate its responsibility. They must, through word and deed, show the people of this country that things can change, and change for the better.

Whither Now?

The *aam aadmi* is aware that the country is being ravaged by the cancer of ineptitude and corruption. The causation of this dreaded disease has been attributed to the exposure the country has had, and continues to have, to the toxic fumes of dishonesty and low moral values emanating from the ruling class and their cohorts. The disease has spread its tentacles into almost every organ of governance and calls for urgent and drastic intervention. Some concerned citizens are convinced that to figure out a cure, a thorough investigation needs to be undertaken by an entity termed 'Lokpal' that will endeavour to locate the sources of this toxicity and put an end to it. The ruling class however strongly objects and claims that with this approach, the cure proposed may be worse than the disease itself. It seems their fear is that if the toxicity is somehow linked to them, they will be quarantined for life.

Right now things are at a stalemate and there appears to be no discernible urgency on anyone's part to attend to the cancer. In the mean time, all one hears are news bulletins informing citizens of the discovery, almost on a daily basis, of additional organs affected by the cancer of corruption.

Does the news affect anybody? Does anyone care?

Fighting for a cause needs an activist
Fighting for change needs a leader

Over the years there have been grass-roots movements led by activists, some peaceful, some militant, that dared to challenge the ruling governments at the centre or state, but they all lacked a pragmatic and coherent vision of what exactly they wanted. For any movement to have a long-term impact, there has to be a visionary whose philosophy and message has to resonate with every section of society, and who should be able to attract hordes of inspired and dedicated foot soldiers to spread that message to every corner of the country.

There is a new political party in town that claims to be the answer to the common man's prayers, and promises corruption-free and people-oriented governance. It has generated a certain level of buzz in the political circles and in the media. It started as a movement by some activists primarily against corruption and then morphed into a political outfit. However, to make a visible impact on the political scene, it will need to overcome its activist mindset and rally around a charismatic leader who can fine-tune a pragmatic and coherent political philosophy that factors in its vision, all aspects of national governance. It will need all the guile to score any sort of victory in a David-and-Goliath contest against the existing powerful and entrenched political parties. If it fails to do so, it will just be another name added to long list of the hundred or so existing political outfits that have been sprouting periodically all over the country in recent years.

How well this new party, the new kid on the block, does, time alone will tell.

'For a successful revolution it is not enough that there is discontent. What is required is a profound and thorough conviction of the justice, necessity and importance of political and social rights.'

—Dr B.R. Ambedkar

Epilogue

Over the years, I have often pondered over what India in the future should look like. Not being a politician, lawyer or constitutional expert, what follows is just a layperson's broad vision and hope.

To start with, there will be a constitutional amendment in place that debars any individual to enter politics at any level even if there is a hint of corruption, anti-social behaviour or any kind of lack of personal integrity. The person will of course have the right to make a representation to the chief election commissioner (CEC) to disprove such allegations. The CEC will in turn exercise his constitutional authority and make a determination independent of any political interference.

At the time of assuming charge of any portfolio at the centre, state or district level, all elected political officials will submit a written affidavit to the prime minister or chief minister, as the case may be, pledging efficiency, honesty and moral integrity in the discharge of their duties. These duties will be spelt out in clear and precise terms in a written format and handed over to the elected official by the appointing authority at the time of the swearing-in ceremony. The list of duties will be in the public domain and displayed on an appropriate website.

The office of Lokpal, as a constitutional authority, will be responsible for ensuring that elected officials perform their responsibilities and take corrective action in case of any wayward behaviour of any such official in consultation with the appointing authority.

No political party will be recognised that has in its manifesto any sort of communal or caste agenda. Any leader who, through word or deed, promotes any kind of blatant divisive or destructive behaviour among his/her followers will be charged with sedition and dealt with expeditiously.

To ensure that the final say on the performance of a government and its elected officials from top to bottom is ultimately judged and decided by 'we the people', the constitution will include a provision of 'general referendum' and a right to recall whenever the people feel the government or officials at any level in power are not acting in their best interest.

The political, bureaucratic, defence, and police power structure will be rationalised to ensure a well-defined and operationally efficient hierarchy that respects the independence of each entity yet shows a cooperative and collective reaction in a crisis.

Combatants, policemen, PWD workers, municipal conservancy staff, or any person whose salary is funded by public money will not be used for personal or domestic purposes by any official.

The terms VIP and VVIP etc. will be discontinued. The practice of using beacons, outriders, and a cavalcade by politicians and other officials is to be restricted only to ceremonial occasions where the dignity of the office is to be reflected. State-provided ceremonial and personal security will be considered only for a limited number of very senior and important functionaries in government.

The Police Force will be reorganised to ensure they meet the needs of the citizens in the twenty-first century. Responding to the needs of the citizens should be their first priority. Political interference at any level will not be tolerated.

Village development, especially in remote areas of the country, will be fast-tracked. Development will be based on a cluster concept with the provision of integrated infrastructure, civic facilities, promotion of local farming and handicrafts and setting up of labour-intensive non-polluting industries.

Availability of affordable housing for citizens will be given top priority. There will be a moratorium on new construction in all cities. All vacant or locked up houses/flats will be bought over by the state at established rates and offered to those seeking affordable housing.* New construction, if permissible, will only be allowed after the inventory bottoms out.

**A recent news item appearing in the Hindustan Times states 62 per cent of India's new housing (almost 11 million units) is vacant.*

Development plans of all urban areas will be put on hold till such time the civic administration has demonstrated that adequate and efficient infrastructure and other civic facilities are in place in the city or town and provisions have been made for the proposed expansion.

Preservation of the environment will be ensured through strict monitoring of green cover, adequate effluent treatment, and elimination of air and water polluting sources. Stiff and swift penalties will be imposed on all polluters.

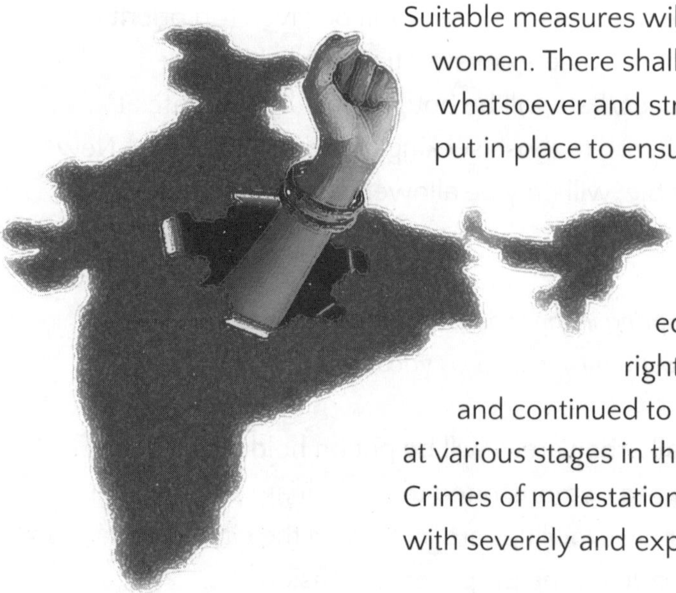

Suitable measures will be taken to empower women. There shall be no discrimination whatsoever and stringent laws will be put in place to ensure their well-being and safety. Gender sensitivity will be introduced in the education of all children right from an early age and continued to be stressed thereafter at various stages in their lives and careers. Crimes of molestation or rape will be dealt with severely and expeditiously.

All educational institutions, public or private, will have the required capacity and facilities as stipulated in the RTE Act. All schools and other public academic institutions will be upgraded and required to impart quality education, especially Maths and English, at all grade levels. Qualification and salaries of teachers will be enhanced to ensure that talented staff are attracted to this profession. Experienced and dedicated educationists will be involved in monitoring the progress of implementation of the RTE Act.

Caste-based or religious discriminations will be considered a serious crime and shall carry severe punishment.

There will be a national minimum wage established for different parts of the country based on categorised skill levels of the various kinds of jobs. People at a higher income level, both in rural and urban areas, will be given tax incentives based on their ability to hire more people or give a better pay benefits package to those employed by them.

Slums and shanty towns will be progressively removed and the people provided with alternative, convenient livable accommodation. Government will review the locations and layouts of the unused defence lands or the obscenely huge colonial-era structures housing political and other functionaries and carve out sections that can be used for the purpose of constructing modest homes for needy slum dwellers.

For the future, it will be the responsibility of sanctioning authorities to ensure that any proposal received for the construction of office, industrial or residential accommodation has in its layout plan a section of the property earmarked for decent accommodation of lower-level workers/domestic staff expected to work in the completed projects.

Any builder who is involved in any illegal or sub-standard construction, or violates the conditions stipulated in the approval accorded for the project, will face a hefty fine, a cancellation of licence. The structure will be demolished and the builder will pay the cost of demolition to the civic authorities. If shoddy construction or poor supervision results in loss of life, appropriate prison term will be given.

If the delay in a trial is due to deliberate stalling tactics by a lawyer or policeman, the judge may decide to include them as accessories to the crime and put them on trial too.

In addition to filing income tax returns, every high-net-worth individual has to file a statement with the Tax authorities giving details of all assets, be they bank accounts, fixed deposits, bonds, shares etc. held anywhere in the world. If on review any discrepancy is discovered, a hefty fine or an automatic prison term kicks in. Also, the source of money for acquisition of fixed assets possessed has to be listed and substantiated, failing which these properties will be seized and auctioned off by the state.

These are just some preliminary thoughts. I'm sure there are many more things that need to be included in the 'vision statement'. Let us hope some day there will emerge a patriotic Indian who will be willing to face the odds and accept the daunting challenge to effect change and take this country forward to the glorious heights of greatness we all desire and deserve.

Jai Hind

The Last Page

I trust the contents of this book have elicited a knowing nod, a smile, or perhaps a burst of laughter from the reader. While critiquing the manuscript, my wife commented, 'Things aren't that bad!' While I may disagree with her assessment, I would love to hear some feel-good news about the country. I look forward to a day when the headlines in newspapers would be:

'All illegal black money stashed abroad recovered. Account holders arrested.'

'Powerful people involved in multi-crore scams thrown in prison. Complaints of chest pains not entertained.'

'All land grabbed from farmers returned. Land sharks convicted and imprisoned.'

'Constitutional amendment to outlaw caste approved unanimously. Equality for all at last.'

'Air, water, and noise pollution at a historic low.'

'Supreme Court declares home ownership for all sections of society, a fundamental right.'

My wish list could go on and on.

We all know that day will never come, and perhaps not much is going to change in the immediate future. On the other hand, maybe we are already at the lowest point of corruption and poor governance in the country. Maybe we have a reason to be upbeat from now on. So, don't yield to despair.

Smile India. Things couldn't possibly get worse